The Wrightsman Lectures I

The Wrightsman Lectures
1964 Rembrandt and the Italian Renaissance
by Kenneth Clark

Rembrandt. Self-portrait at the age of 34. *National Gallery*

Kenneth Clark

Rembrandt
and the Italian Renaissance

The Wrightsman Lectures

Institute of Fine Arts, New York University, 1964

Delivered at The Metropolitan Museum of Art, New York, N.Y.

New York University Press

*This is the first volume
of The Wrightsman Lectures,
which are delivered annually
under the auspices of the
New York University Institute of Fine Arts*

Library of Congress Catalog No. 66–13550
Published in England by John Murray Ltd.
Composed and printed by J. J. Augustin, Glückstadt, West Germany
Bound by Quinn & Boden Company, Inc., Rahway, New Jersey
First impression

Foreword

While lecturing on Rembrandt at Oxford in 1947 I began to realise how deeply he understood and profited from the art of the Italian Renaissance, and in particular that of the Quattrocento; and some years later I put together a few of my conclusions in a paper presented to Professor Johannes Wilde on his sixtieth birthday. I am not a specialist in Dutch art and had no thought of expanding or publishing this material; but when Mr. Charles Wrightsman asked me to give the first of a series of lectures with which he had endowed New York University, and expressed the hope that I would speak about Rembrandt, I thought that my twenty-five-year-old speculations might stand development. Whether or not I was right the reader can judge.

I must record my deep gratitude to Mr. and Mrs. Wrightsman and to the University, not only for the honour they did me in asking me to give the lectures, but also because their choice of subject gave me the opportunity, which my scruples as an art-historian would not otherwise have allowed, of spending two years in the company of this marvellous genius, whose greatness, both as an artist and a human being, cannot be appreciated without close daily intimacy.

Dutch art historians will, I am sure, find much to criticise in this book; but to approach a great national figure from a new direction can sometimes be of value, and I hope that a certain familiarity with Italian art has allowed me to make confrontations which might not have occurred to specialists. In order to make these comparisons as specific as possible I have made frequent references to the inventory of Rembrandt's possessions drawn up in 1656 at the time of his *cessio bonorum*. No complete English translation of this fascinating document exists, and I have therefore added one as an appendix.

My thanks are due to Professor Johannes Wilde, who helped me with references to Italian art, and to Mr. Frits Lugt, the doyen of Rembrandt Studies, who allowed me to discuss some of my problems with him. I must also record my gratitude to Mr. Craig Hugh Smyth, and other members of the Institute of Fine Art of New York University, who received me so hospitably in the Spring of 1964 when I was giving these lectures.

Saltwood, 1965   K. C.

vi

Contents

List of Plates

175. Marten de Vos. *Remissionem Peccatorum*. Engraving. *British Museum.*

176. Marcantonio after Raphael. Parnassus. Engraving. *British Museum.*

177. Raphael. St. Paul Preaching at Ephesus. Tempera on paper. *Victoria & Albert Museum, London.*

178. Donatello. The Ascension (detail). Marble. *Victoria & Albert Museum, London.*

179. Masaccio. St. Peter's Shadow Healing the Sick. Fresco. *Santa Maria del Carmine, Florence.*

180. Rembrandt. The Return of the Prodigal Son. Canvas. *The Hermitage, Leningrad.*

181. Early Christian. Adoration of the Magi. Ivory. *British Museum.*

My thanks are due to the following museums, galleries and collectors, who have allowed me to reproduce pictures in their collections. I am particularly grateful to those who have waived any reproduction fee:

Albertina, Vienna; Art Institute, Chicago; Ashmolean Museum, Oxford; Bamberg Cathedral; Barber Institute of Fine Arts, Birmingham; Brera, Milan; British Museum; Ducal Palace, Vienna; His Grace the Duke of Devonshire, Chatsworth; Ecole des Beaux-Arts, Paris; Fitzwilliam Museum, Cambridge, England; Fogg Art Museum, Harvard University; Frick Collection, New York; Groningen, Holland; Gulbenkian Foundation, Lisbon; ex Harewood Collection; The Hermitage, Leningrad; Hessisches Landesmuseum, Darmstadt; Kenwood House, London; Kramarski Collection, New York; Kunsthalle, Hamburg; Lehman Collection, New York; Louvre, Paris; Lugt Collection, Institut Neerlandais, Paris; Mauritshuis, The Hague; Metropolitan Museum, New York; Museum of Fine Arts, Budapest; National Gallery, London; National Museum, Stockholm; National Gallery, of Art Washington; Marquis of Normanby Collection; Norton Simon Foundation, Los Angeles; Pierpont Morgan Library, New York; Prado, Madrid; Pushkin Museum, Moscow; Oskar Reinhart Collection, Winterthur; Rijksmuseum, Amsterdam; Six Collection, Amsterdam; Speelman Collection, London; Staatliche Kunstsammlungen, Cassel; Staatlichen Kunstsammlungen, Dresden; Staatsgemäldesammlungen, Munich; Städelsches Kunstinstitut, Frankfurt a. M.; State Museum, Berlin-Dahlem; Teyler Museum, Haarlem; Uffizi, Florence; van Beuningen Collection, Museum Boymans, Rotterdam; Victoria and Albert Museum, London; von Hirsch Collection, Basle; Windsor Castle Library.

Paintings and drawings in the Royal Collection are produced by gracious permission of Her Majesty the Queen.

Paintings and drawings from the National Gallery are produced by courtesy of the Trustees of The National Gallery, London.

The drawing by Polidoro da Caravaggio of The Entombment is produced by courtesy of the Fogg Art Museum, Harvard University, Meta and Paul J. Sachs Collection.

The painting The Polish Rider is copyright The Frick Collection, New York.

The drawing Manoah's Sacrifice is copyright F. Lugt.

1

The Anti-Classical Rembrandt

In the year 1620, when the youthful Rembrandt went to the University of Leyden, Dutch painting might have seemed, to the outside observer, to be profoundly and almost incurably provincial. Indeed, my words "Dutch painting" give a false impression, for each of the leading cities of the United Provinces, Haarlem, Leyden, Utrecht and so forth, had its own school, with its own line of business from which the local masters seldom departed. A Dutch patron looked to one or other of the schools for the kind of painting he required: modest, complacent portraiture, detailed still life (with, as often as not, a moral attached), and quasi-topographical landscape. The more cultivated patrons recognised that great art existed beyond their borders in Venice, Rome and Bologna, and even in Flanders, where, since 1610, the fame of Rubens had been established; and they applauded those of their countrymen who had been bold enough to attempt an international style, especially the Utrecht painters Honthorst and Terbrugghen who had learnt the exciting new tricks of Caravaggio. They also praised, though with less conviction, the attempts of an Amsterdam painter, Pieter Lastman, to practise the kind of historical painting by which, according to the theorists, art could become respectable. But in their attempt to push their local painting into the mainstream of traditional art, Dutch connoisseurs were hampered, as the English were hampered two hundred years later, by the convictions of a protestant, democratic community. The Church could no longer patronise art directly and protestantism had not formed an iconography to put in place of the fleshly splendours and afflictions of the counter-reformation. State patronage, without the wilful taste of an individual autocrat, was as half-hearted then as it is today. It is true that the newly rich bourgeoisie were keen to form collections, but their taste in contemporary paintings was not of a kind to change the domestic character of Dutch art. Looking at the scene in 1620 an intelligent critic might have predicted a Jan Steen or a Hobbema; but he could hardly have imagined that one of his countrymen might achieve the peculiar greatness of a Titian or a Donatello, that quality which Matthew Arnold called "high seriousness," and which, in the art of painting, seemed to be reserved for those brought up in a tradition of monumental religious art, with its roots in Mediterranean antiquity.

This miracle took place; it was achieved by Rembrandt, and, in the chapters that follow, I shall try to show what lay behind his achievement. To his extraordinary powers of hand and eye and "rightly judging human heart," Rembrandt added certain unexpected qualities that long passed unrecognised: a deep sympathy for all that was greatest in European art; an excavator's instinct which could lead him back through the stylistic accretions of over a century and an intellectual understanding of the means by which the masters of the classical tradition had achieved their effects. All great artists have studied the work of their predecessors and borrowed from it, if they have felt the need; but few have ranged so widely, or shown such powers of assimilation as Rembrandt. He is the supreme self-educator. By rare good fortune we can follow him in his study of the classical tradition almost as closely as Professor Livingstone Lowes could follow Coleridge on the road to Xanadu. And just as no one, I suppose, has thought the less of Coleridge's poetic powers because he took facts and even phrases from the diaries of old explorers, so no one, I trust, will find his admiration for Rembrandt diminished by the knowledge of what he owed to Raphael, Mantegna and Leonardo da Vinci. In fact Rembrandt, by the force of his imagination, reshaped so completely the pictorial ideas and motives which he took from earlier painters that we could not have recognised them without intermediate stages which reveal their gradual transformation. In Rembrandt's re-interpretation of the art of the past we can see something that went far beyond even the most intelligent study, some intuitive sympathy with the form-creating energies of earlier epochs, that allowed him to dig out of his imagination ancient motives which he had never seen.

2

Fig. 1. Rembrandt. Judas Returning the Thirty Pieces of Silver

In the main, however, this book is about a more demonstrable subject, the manner in which Rembrandt transformed his style by the study of Italian renaissance art; and I must therefore begin by describing the character of this style which was to be so drastically altered. His original, inborn talents were recognised very early in his career, and his contemporaries described them so emphatically that they continued to be accepted in critical literature for over two hundred years. In a series of personal notes written about the year 1630 Constantin Huygens, a distinguished scholar and connoisseur, committed himself to the extravagant opinion that "the miller's son Rembrandt and the embroiderer's son Lievens were already on a par with the most famous painters, and would soon surpass them." And there follows the critical comment that Rembrandt excelled in judgement and liveliness of emotional expression whereas Lievens excelled in invention, in a certain boldness of subject and grandeur of form.[1] This well-known statement, often quoted to show the

Fig. 2. Rembrandt. Self-portrait. [Etching]

fallibility of contemporary judgements, has a peculiar interest in our present context. In Huygens' opinion it was clearly Lievens who was destined to restore to Dutch art the grandeur of the great traditions, whereas Rembrandt was above all a lively illustrator. And to prove his point he cites a picture of Judas returning the thirty pieces of silver in which, he claims, Rembrandt has surpassed any Italian or ancient painter. The picture, now in the Normanby Collection (fig. 1) is not the kind of Rembrandt most admired today. The design is unsteady, the sense of space is confusing, and the forms themselves are hard to grasp. But it remains a memorable instance of *affectuum vivacitate*. The gesture and expression of the Judas made him a symbol of agony of mind which was engraved and reproduced in several other contexts during the 1630's,[2] and the reactions of the priests, horrified, hypocritical and apprehensive are also marvellously observed. Behind it lie studies of grimace and gesture, made with exceptional powers of memory and concentration on a fleeting moment. We know from Rembrandt's early etchings that one of his chief exercises was the observation of his own face in a mirror, expressing every violent emotion which he was likely to need in his narrative pictures (fig. 2); and amongst his drawings are snapshots of pain and anger done with a kind of fury (fig. 3) for which it is hard to think of a precedent.[3]

4

Fig. 3. Rembrandt. Jacob Being Shown Joseph's Coat.
[Drawing]

These drawings and etchings, even more than the paintings, show the talents which contemporaries recognised in the young painter of Leyden: narrative invention, a sense of movement, and a gift for conveying violent emotion by a violently unorthodox style. Strangely enough, in the 1620's a young Dutch artist with these rebellious leanings was by no means debarred from official patronage. There still existed, left over from the first years of the century, a taste for violence and excess; the horrors of the Jacobean stage were, after all, only ten or fifteen years old. Constantine Huygens himself, although a man of great classical culture, was not at all a conventional classicist. He admired Rubens, and praised in particular the vivid horrors of his Medusa; he translated Donne's poems into Dutch; he had a copy of Shakespeare's works in his library, and could have sympathised with the disillusioned and savage view of antiquity in *Troilus and Cressida* or *Timon of Athens*. Thus Rembrandt's most enlightened early patron was not the man to restrain the natural anti-classicism of this young rebel.

Fig. 4. Rembrandt. Self-portrait. [Drawing]

It is sometimes said that the character of Rembrandt as the rebel artist is an invention of romanticism; and it is true that during the nineteenth century the Rembrandt legend, especially the story of his fall from popularity and social ostracism, was given more dramatic colouring. But that the young man from Leyden saw himself as a tough and rebellious character is made perfectly clear to us in a whole series of self-portraits. The earliest of these, a drawing in the British Museum (fig. 4), is the very image of a rebel, with thick lips and strawberry nose; and the earliest etching, done about a year later, is scarcely more refined, the truculent expression

6

being rendered by an equally bold and truculent line. Most conclusive of all is the etching where he has portrayed himself as one of his favourite beggars snarling at the prosperous, bourgeois society which was shortly to welcome him so warmly (fig. 5). This angry impatience with convention was a fundamental part of Rembrandt's character, and although he managed to control it during his years of prosperity, it came out strongly in his middle life and is emphasised in the three early biographies written by men who had first-hand information about him.[4]

But side by side with this rebelliousness was an immense seriousness; nor should we be right in thinking that the young rough-neck was an un-educated boor. The regulations of the Latin School in Leyden which Rembrandt attended laid down that pupils should read Cicero's letters and speeches, the plays of Terence, the poetry of Ovid, Virgil, and Horace

Fig. 5. Rembrandt. A Peasant Seated. [Etching]

and the histories of Caesar, Sallust, and Livy:[5] all this *before* entering the University, which at that time had as high a standard of learning as any in northern Europe. When, therefore, we find Rembrandt illustrating a classical legend in an unorthodox manner, this is not through ignorance. More likely he has read the text with particular care and in doing so has seen through the conventional representations of academism. An example is the Rape of Proserpine (fig. 7), perhaps his earliest important commission, for it seems to have been painted for Prince Frederick of Orange. The design goes back to a classical original known in several sarcophagi. But although Rembrandt was later to become a student and collector of antique sculpture, at this date he had probably absorbed the idea via Rubens, whose lost picture[6] of the subject could have been known to him in an engraving by Soutman (fig. 6).

Fig. 6. Soutman, after Rubens. The Rape of Proserpine

Rembrandt has made an oblong composition into an upright one and placed the plunging horse, rather unfunctionally, below Pluto's chariot; he has retained, even strengthened the ascending diagonal line (in this he is nearer to the sarcophagus than to Rubens); but when it came to the actual group his sense of truth would not allow him to accept the in-

8

Fig. 7. Rembrandt. The Rape of Proserpine

effectual eloquence of those flung-back arms, with which, by classical convention, Sabine women and other heroines of antique legend convey the information that they are being raped. What in fact would a decent young Dutch girl do in the situation? Kick and scratch: scratch his eyes out. This Proserpine is doing, so effectively that the swarthy, oriental Pluto has turned away his head in alarm. Wholly unclassical. Of course, this kind of realism alone could have been merely vulgar and distracting; but Rembrandt has understood something of the mystery of this legend, and has conveyed it by a magic-working use of light and shade so that his picture, if not the philosophical myth of Eleusis, is, as Dr. Saxl has said, a "cosmic fairy tale."[7] Incidentally, this is the kind of Rembrandt which by its jewel-like colour and breathless plunges from light to dark enchanted the painters of the eighteenth century, so that, with a few changes of detail, it could easily become an episode in a fête at Rambouillet.

Unfortunately, most of the other examples of Rembrandt's anti-classical independence are not as pleasing. In fact they are, to our eyes, some of the most unpleasing, not to say disgusting, pictures ever produced by a great artist. But they were admired in their own day, and even for us they achieve a kind of horrible fascination from the very violence of his reaction against the conventions of ideal art.

Fig. 8. Rembrandt.
Woman Seated on a Mound. [Etching]

Fig. 9. Rembrandt.
Diana Bathing. [Etching]

10

Fig. 10. Rembrandt. Study for Diana Bathing. [Drawing]

The first of these conventions which, by 1600, seemed to lie at the centre of all civilised design, was the nude. Rembrandt thought that the stream-lined goddesses of Bloemaert or Goltzius with their tiny heads and tapering limbs did not exist (they are in fact extremely rare),[8] and in his indignation at this piece of imposture he set out to show what the average woman with no clothes on was really like. I think he rather overstated his case; but apparently his contemporaries did not think so, for his etching of a naked woman seated on a mound (fig. 8) had an immediate success, and was copied by Hollar for further circulation. He followed this protest against the nude in general with a more pointed blow at the nudity of classical goddesses, in an etching of Diana bathing (fig. 9). We can tell that Rembrandt meant to give us a shock because in his original drawing for the etching, done from a model, the body is less flabby and collapsed (fig. 10). In the etching he has

11

added all the small furrows which an elaborate, habitual costume—garters, stays, sleeve-bands—leave on the soft surface of the flesh, and has thus avoided the streamlining which all his life he had hated. The moral is clear. Goddesses are ordinary women, and ordinary women had better not take their clothes off. I should add that this point of view, although acceptable in the 1630's, became, as Dutch society acquired a smoother polish, one of the chief criticisms levelled against him. By 1671 Jan de Bisschop, a talented painter, whose drawings of landscapes are still confused with Rembrandt's own, expressed his shame at the sight of a Leda or a Danae painted with a fat swollen belly, pendulous breasts and garter marks on her legs. He was obviously thinking of Rembrandt; and, ten years later, Andries Pels in a poem in which he called Rembrandt the "first heretic in the art of painting" (*de erste ketter in de Schilderkunst*) repeats the same list of objectionable characteristics, including the garter marks, which have since become almost symbols of Rembrandt's anti-classicism.

Another symbol, even more repulsive, occurs in his etching of the Good Samaritan (fig. 11), dated in the fourth state 1633. It is Rembrandt's dogmatic sermon against the frivolity of elegance. The forms are not simply ungraceful; they are reduced to clouts and clods. The figures hang from one another like a string of potatoes, and their sequence of lumpish shapes comes most sharply into focus with the dog, who is there to remind us that if we are to practise the Christian virtues of charity and humility, we must extend our sympathy to all natural functions, even those which disgust us. It is interesting that almost the only person to recognise the meaning of this etching was Goethe, in his essay *Rembrandt als Denker*. As a matter of fact, the dog seems to be an after-thought, for it does not appear in the small oil painting in the Wallace Collection, which I believe to be an authentic *modello* for the etching; and scholars jealous for Rembrandt's good name have tried to maintain that it was added by a pupil.

The most disturbing and the most unforgettable of Rembrandt's anti-classical paintings is the Rape of Ganymede (1635), now in the gallery at Dresden (fig. 12). It is a protest not only against antique art, but against antique morality, and against the combination of the two in sixteenth-century Rome. What led him to choose this subject in the first place? Obviously he must have seen some sixteenth century representation of the subject, and I think this was almost certainly a rather

Fig. 11. Rembrandt. The Good Samaritan. [Etching]

crude engraving after Michelangelo by Nicolo Barbizet (fig. 13).[8a] The original drawing was one of the series made by Michelangelo for his friend Tomaso Cavalieri; it is now lost, but is known to us from a copy in the Fogg Museum.[9] This copy shows that the dog, unexpectedly, was part of Michelangelo's original design; and in its cruder form in the engraving it is remarkably similar to the dog in the Good Samaritan, and wears the same spiky collar. It would be ironical if this most unideal addition to the etching were to have been ultimately derived from Michelangelo. We may guess that Rembrandt's feelings were divided between admiration for the design of the Ganymede with its acroterian eagle filling the sky, and a protestant-Christian revulsion against the sexual practices of paganism that Michelangelo's version so clearly implies: for Rembrandt never looked at a motive without pondering on the full implications of the sub-

13

Fig. 12. Rembrandt. The Rape of Ganymede

Fig. 13. Nicole Barbizet after Michelangelo. Ganymede. [Engraving]

ject. Michelangelo and Rembrandt are the two most profoundly moral of great artists; but Michelangelo's morality with its concordance of Platonic and Augustinian ethics, was of a complexity which Rembrandt could neither penetrate nor accept.[10] I think that Rembrandt was shocked, and he was determined that his picture should shock. But at the same time he could not resist the motive; and, as usual, he began to ask himself what the episode could really have been like. Well, he had seen a naughty child snatched up by its mother in very much the attitude of Michelangelo's

15

Fig. 14. Rembrandt. The Naughty Child. [Drawing]

Fig. 15. Rembrandt. Study for the Ganymede. [Drawing]

Ganymede, and had delighted in its display of uninhibited rage (fig. 14).
Perhaps he had seen a similar episode with the child turned backwards
on; or perhaps he knew some representation (he could not have known
the original) of a splendid Titianesque design now in the National Gallery, London[11]: at any rate he was fascinated by the bold curves of
stomach and bottom, and a drawing, also in Dresden (fig. 15), shows that
at an early stage he made these interlocking forms the nub of his design.
As a plastic idea it is magnificent: but by showing the physical conse-
quences of Ganymede's fear Rembrandt has gone out of his way to make
it repulsive. In this he differs from the mildly unclassical realism of, say,
Velasquez's Mars; still more from the realism of Caravaggio, whose Amor,
also derived from Michelangelo's Ganymede, with the eagle's wings

Fig. 16. Polidoro da Caravaggio. Amor

sprouting from the boy's own shoulders, retains the shameless physical arrogance of antiquity (fig. 16). In the end I am not certain which of the two images is more repulsive; but there is no doubt that Rembrandt's image gains immense power from his struggle against the potent charm of classic art. It is like one of those blasphemies which precede conversion.

At some date in the early 1630's Rembrandt received an important commission from the head of the Dutch state, Prince Frederick Henry. This was for a series of pictures of the Passion to hang in his chapel; five of them survive and are in the gallery at Munich. The commission was almost certainly arranged by Huygens, as Rembrandt wrote to him a number of letters of gratitude, in which, incidentally, he seems to experience no difficulty in employing the elaborate language of flunkeydom used by artists in addressing their patrons until the time of Courbet. Rembrandt worked on the series for six or seven years and, when delivering two of the latest in 1639, he included an explanation of why, as he puts it, "these pictures had remained so long under my hands." It is because he had been trying to achieve what he called *die meeste ende die naetureelste be-weechgelickheyt*. I quote these words in Dutch because even Dutch scholars are not agreed as to what they mean. I should have translated them "the greatest degree of natural movement," but Dr. van Gelder has given reasons why they could mean the greatest inward emotion. In either case, they imply that Rembrandt was still following the same course as he had done ten years earlier, when Huygens had so greatly admired his picture of Judas. Of course it is possible that these words were written to please

Fig. 17. Rembrandt. The Resurrection

Huygens and support the flattering tone of the letter. In one of the pictures he sent, the Resurrection (fig. 17), the discomfiture of the soldiers is depicted with a grotesque violence which shows no advance upon the early 1630's, and personally I believe that the date of 1639 was added at the last moment. It gives many indications of having lain under his hand for several years. The other picture of 1639, the Entombment

Fig. 18. Rembrandt. The Entombment

(fig. 18), shows that Rembrandt had already passed into a different phase, both of feeling and design, which justifies Dr. van Gelder's interpretation of *naetureelste beweechgelickheyt*.

While the commission dragged on and (we may guess) caused him considerable annoyance, Rembrandt contrived an enormous present for his patron. Knowing Huygens' taste for violence and horrors, he determined to go to the limit. The result was a picture about 10 feet long by 8 feet high of the Blinding of Samson (fig. 19). Huygens apparently declined this embarrassing gift; but Rembrandt stuck to his point and a few weeks afterwards wrote another obsequious letter in which he says, "even against my Lord's wishes I send you the accompanying canvas, hoping that you will not mistrust my motives, because it is the first token I offer my Lord". He added, "My Lord, hang this piece in a strong light, so that it may best vouch for itself". The evidence is not quite conclusive, but on the whole it looks as if Huygens got the Samson after all. The Blinding of Samson is an extremely disturbing picture. Only a man of genius could have done

20

Fig. 19. Rembrandt. The Blinding of Samson

anything so consistently horrifying. Apart from the revolting realism of the actual blinding, every detail, every hand and foot, is ugly in itself. The silhouette of the man on the left has the same character as the dog in the Good Samaritan. His trousers are like the most hideous legs of Jacobean sideboards. The man brandishing the sword on the left is as grotesque as the guards in the Resurrection. But as a feat of pictorial imagination it is appallingly effective. A wave of light, which seems to have burst through a broken dam, overwhelms the miserable Samson, and then is gone from him for ever. And the figures of his tormentors are inventions of great dramatic power. The grotesque halberdier, pointing his weapon at the fallen giant like a stoker[12], looks at his victim with a startled compassion; he has the shagginess and complexity of the north. But the men who bind Samson and put out his eyes are from the south, are, in fact, reminiscences of the guards in Raphael's Liberation of St. Peter, and they are concentrating relentlessly on their task.

For Rembrandt the painting of Samson was therapeutic. In following the development of his mind, one feels that at certain points he has to get things out of his system. Here he has worked off all the need to make a violent impact by the portrayal of expression, which was part of his revolt against the smooth and restrained gestures of classicism. In fact he never ceased to be passionately interested in the emotions revealed by the human face; but thenceforward he set about conveying them more subtly.

I have used the word Jacobean in speaking of Huygens' taste, and I may repeat it now; the Samson has some of the bloodthirsty confusion of a Jacobean play. Its style is frequently described as Baroque, but the abruptness of the transitions, the absence of flowing movement, the uneasy fragmentation of area are all contrary to true Baroque. I am, of course, using the word Baroque in a stylistic rather than chronological sense. A number of styles flourished and competed in the early seventeenth century, and to group them all under the heading Baroque, as is sometimes done, is to impoverish our already limited vocabulary of critical terms. The word should, I believe, be limited to the international style which manifested itself in Lanfranco, Pietro da Cortona, the mature Rubens and ultimately Bernini. I need not enumerate its characteristics. The feeling for continuous movement, extending from the parts to the whole composition; the command of surging masses, passing in and out of light and shade; the convention-

Fig. 20. Rembrandt. Samson and Delilah

alised imagery, the theatrical gestures; the use of curves, the diagonal recession, the emotive use of light and shade: all these have been repeatedly analysed and expounded during the last fifty years. By about 1625, when Lanfranco had succeeded Domenichino in S. Andrea della Valle, we can say that Bolognese classicism had turned into a sort of official Baroque, a style less exciting than the all-out Baroque of Rubens and Pietro da Cortona, but also much more suitable as a basis for academism.

This style was fundamentally distasteful to Rembrandt. He disliked the rhetorical imagery, the standardised types and the sinuous design. Correggio, who is from so many points of view the forerunner of Baroque, is an artist at the opposite pole to Rembrandt. Nevertheless Rembrandt recognised that Baroque was the triumphant international style of the time. It was the style of Rubens, whose unchallenged success, not only in Flanders but in Holland, was constantly in Rembrandt's mind in the 1630's. To make his way as a painter of histories a northern artist had at least to speak the same language, and this, by some means which is not easily explained, Rembrandt succeeded in doing. At the surprisingly early date of 1628 he painted a picture which passes a strict definition of Baroque on almost every count, the Samson and Delilah in Berlin (fig. 20). Here are the twist, the recession, the passage in and out of light and shade—all the characteristics which had only recently been perfected in Italian painting. Even the imagery is more or less baroque, although the Macbeth-like figure[13] in the background would have been too uncouth for Guercino or Cerano.[14]

During the next fifteen years Rembrandt executed three or four pictures, and at least three large etchings, in what may properly be called the Baroque style. In these he employed the technical devices of the style, without ever quite assimilating the imagery. He even did several works in which he exploited the Catholic sentiment of the high Baroque, with some of its attendant artificialities. We must not think him insincere in doing so. This was an age of religious confusion when serious men, in their search for truth, changed their beliefs in what seems to us (who have no beliefs) an irresponsible manner. For example, the great Dutch poet Vondel, who was an ardent Catholic, was for a time a practising Mennonite. Rembrandt's mother was born a Catholic, and still read her breviary when Rembrandt painted her. He was baptised into the official Calvinist Church,

Fig. 21. Rembrandt. The Death of the Virgin. [Etching]

but in the 1630's seems to have been chiefly in the company of Arminian Remonstrants. Later he was in sympathy with the Mennonites, although never officially a member of their congregation. Through all these changes of religious inclination he remained essentially Protestant in spirit; but he knew what Catholicism meant, and I do not doubt that when he did his etching of the Death of the Virgin dated 1639 (fig. 21) he was trying quite

Fig. 22. Rembrandt. The Death of the Virgin (detail). [Etching]

sincerely to produce the kind of work which would satisfy Catholic sentiment in Amsterdam—we may say which *had* satisfied, because his treatment
of the subject is based on a window in the Old Church of Amsterdam by
Dirk Crabeth. From the point of view of picture-making he has gone the
whole way. He has even accepted the baroque convention that the roof of
Our Lady's bedroom would open to admit clouds and light and a few
rather rustic angels. But when he comes to the figure of the dying woman,
this is too serious a matter to be treated rhetorically; and instead of an
idealised head with upturned eyes, he gives the misery of extreme sickness.
The Virgin (fig. 22)—no doubt inspired by Saskia, who in course of four
difficult confinements spent much of her time in bed—is too weak to raise
her head, but one of the apostles does so, with his hand behind the pillow,
and with the other hand wipes the sweat from her upper lip. What could
be further from ideal art? Except, perhaps, the apostle who checks her
pulse by looking at his watch. The Death of the Virgin is a full, generous,

26

warm-hearted work, but compared with Rembrandt's later etchings, it suffers from the incompatability of two styles; or perhaps we may say that the real Rembrandt, who is revealed in the touching figure of the Virgin, or the sublime invention of the two women at the foot of the bed, cannot address us directly, as he would wish to do, with all these declamatory clouds about. Most of the figures are, in fact, completely un-baroque; the kneeling woman has the austere truthfulness of the early Renaissance, and the St. John has been frequently, I think groundlessly, claimed as a derivation from Mantegna. The same difficulty is presented in very simple terms by the etching of the Virgin and Child in the Clouds (fig. 23). If the Virgin had been on the ground all would have been well. Then she could have

Fig. 23. Rembrandt. The Virgin in the Clouds. [Etching]

looked down on her plain little Dutch pigmy infant. But being in the clouds, she has had to turn her head to heaven, a posture derived from an antique Niobe, and repeated by a sequence of painters from Raphael to Guido Reni. This kind of stylistic refinement, departing at every stage further from the original impression, was quite foreign to Rembrandt. His Madonna, a truthful record of the life around him, is not transported to another world, and the realism of her head contradicts its artificial inclination.

The impossibility of combining plain truth with baroque rhetoric was no doubt one of the chief reasons that led Rembrandt to develop a means of presentation which I may call classic. This word, too, I am using in a stylistic rather than a chronological sense, Wölfflin's sense rather than Burckhardt's. Classic art aims at clarity and economy, both in presentation of subject and in design; and in order to achieve this clarity, forms are either arranged parallel with the picture plane or united in a finite and comprehensible space. Lines are continued in order to maintain the stability of the whole composition. Figures do not overlap, and as far as possible each form preserves its identity so that the spectator can understand its structure immediately.

The extent to which classic discipline altered Rembrandt's sense of design may be seen by comparing two famous etchings of more or less the same subject—Christ Presented to the People. The first, dated 1635 (fig. 24), the year of the Blinding of Samson, is, from the dramatic point of view, an extraordinary work. The character of Pilate is worthy of Balzac. Evidently the type of a well-meaning colonial administrator, half-way between a civil servant and a retired general, has not changed greatly since Rembrandt's day, and the futile, depreciatory gesture with which he attempts to restrain the angry priests is perfectly observed. The priests themselves are marvellous studies in *odium theologicum*, hypocrisy, fanaticism, senile obstinacy and care for vested interests being vividly represented. Huygens' *affectuum vivacitate* could hardly go further. But when I cease to read the plate like a novel and think of the design, I suffer a real sense of discomfort. It is an example of what I have called Rembrandt's Jacobean Baroque, and is of course designed to lead the eye in a series of curves up to the somewhat sentimental figure of Christ (taken directly from Guido Reni). But the twisting, conical movement is so often interrupted and

28

Fig. 24. Rembrandt. Christ before Pilate (1635). [Etching]

broken by incidents and details that it never surges upward as a true baroque design would do. No doubt this is partly the fault of the medium— or rather of Rembrandt's misuse of the medium, for in this case he has carried his etching as far as a mezzotint. The oil sketch in the National Gallery, London, is far more successful in the massing of light and shade. But the fact remains that at this date Rembrandt's attempt to give to his compositions the flow and sweep of the Baroque often ended in restlessness and instability, and even the actual forms have a curiously unstructural character, like damp dish-cloths.

In the etching of 1655 (fig. 25) he has gone to the opposite extreme. So great is his desire for clarity and order that the main lines have been drawn with a ruler. The Mondrian-like rectangles are presented to us flat on, like a grandiose modern set on rather a shallow stage, with a careful suggestion of perspective in the wings.[15] We feel that it should have been some monumental wall painting, some fresco which, for grandeur and solemnity of design, could bear comparison with Masaccio or Raphael.[16] In this austere setting the literary content is of secondary importance. Of course, anything that Rembrandt does is crammed with humanity; but the Dickensian contrast of satire and sentiment has vanished. The high priest is a dignified character, not without a certain pathos, as of one who unwillingly fulfils his destiny; Christ views the crowd with a strange detachment and makes no direct appeal to our emotions; and only one figure, the deboshed youth with plumes in his hat, who stands to the left, is a relic of Rembrandt's early love of the grotesque.

Contrasts of this kind can be found repeatedly in Rembrandt's drawings and etchings, and they show one of the most sustained and calculated reformations of design ever achieved by a great painter. The strange thing is that until quite recently the intellectual power and classicism of his later works were completely ignored. None of his contemporaries seem to have been aware of it, and nineteenth-century writers on Rembrandt did not recognise its significance. The reasons for this are twofold; first the prejudices created by the early literary sources of Rembrandt's life and art; and secondly the fact that whereas Rembrandt's sense of design underwent a drastic change, his imagery remained more or less the same, and it is by his imagery that the majority of people, even the majority of art historians, assess the personality of a painter.

We have at least three biographies of Rembrandt by men who had either known him or had known his pupils, and they all agree in stressing his radical anti-classicism. The first is by Joachim von Sandrart, a courtly, much-travelled hack, who was exactly Rembrandt's age, and had known him personally in Amsterdam from 1637 to 1642. By 1675, when he published his famous book on painting known as the *Teutsche Academie* (the actual title is twenty-four lines long), he had forgotten much of what he

30

Fig. 25. Rembrandt. Christ Presented to the People (1655). [Etching, 1st state]

had learnt and he makes a number of mistakes of fact. But the general impression remained, and had lost nothing in thirty years spent as a court painter and academician. Rembrandt was an ignorant man who "had not visited Italy or other places where the Antique and Theory of Art may be studied; a defect all the more serious since he could but poorly read Netherlandish, and thus profit little from books. He remained ever faithful to the conventions adopted by him, and did not hesitate to oppose and contradict our rules of art, such as anatomy and the proportions of the human body, perspective and the usefulness of classical statues, Raphael's drawings and judicious pictorial disposition and the academies, which are so particularly necessary for our profession." And the reason for this was largely in his character, for "he did not know in the least how to keep his station, and always associated with the lower orders, whereby he was hampered in his work. He painted few subjects from classical poetry, alle-

31

gories or striking historical scenes, but mostly subjects that are ordinary and without special significance, but pleasing to him because they were picturesque" (if that be a fair translation of the word *schilderachtig*). This famous judgement is demonstrably incorrect in every detail but one, and we may ask how Sandrart was able to impose it on posterity. The answer is suggested by the next short biography of Rembrandt, by the Florentine art-historian Filippo Baldinucci, which was based on the information of a Danish painter named Bernardt Keil who was Rembrandt's pupil from 1642 to 1644: "the ugly and plebeian face by which he was ill-favoured," says Baldinucci, "was accompanied by untidy and dirty clothes, since it was his custom, when working, to wipe his brushes on himself, and to do other things of a similar nature. When he was at work he would not have granted an audience to the first monarch in the world." This is the kind of human touch we all enjoy and it is not surprising that early estimates of Rembrandt's art are strongly coloured by accounts of his social habits. And in the seventeenth century they had a sociological importance, for they seemed to be a betrayal of everything that respectable artists had striven for and achieved during the last hundred and fifty years. Vasari, writing to Vincenzo Borghini in 1566, says, "I have lived to see art rise suddenly and free herself from knavery and beastliness". The artist had suddenly become clean and polite, the friend or, at least, the humble, obedient servant of princes.

Rembrandt was none of these things, and it followed that his art must also be lacking in the academic virtues. His biographers found support for this view in Rembrandt's early works, the anti-academic pictures and etchings, which, even today, give us something of a shock. These were the works by which he was generally known up to the end of the nineteenth century. Houbraken, author of the longest of the early lives, containing judgements which are far from foolish, cites almost nothing but early paintings, although the pupils from whom he derived his information (he wrote in 1715) must have been working with Rembrandt during his later period. And in one respect, as I have said, Sandrart's criticism was justified. Rembrandt, who came to accept so much of classical art, never accepted the classical proportions of the human figure[17] for either the male or the female nude. His drawings of the nude became less provocatively monstrous; many of them, indeed, are quite seductive, and when his model is a young

Fig. 26. Rembrandt. Reclining Model. [Drawing]

girl the result is almost like a Manet (fig. 26). But the abstract system which antique art had imposed on the human body he would not admit. It violated two of his deepest beliefs: the uniqueness of the individual and the humility of our mortal state.

As to my second point, the persistence of an anti-academic strain in Rembrandt's images: we may agree that the more deliberately shocking elements—the Ganymede, the dog, the halberdier in the Blinding of Samson—were dropped. There is an immense change in the direction of quietness and solemnity. Even such villainous figures as the high priest who presents Christ to the people, or the disgraced Haman in the Hermitage picture, are treated with sympathy and restraint. "In tragic life, God wot, no villain need be." And yet Rembrandt's imagery remains profoundly unclassical and, to an academic eye, grotesque. Two examples will illustrate this point. The first is a small etching which he did in 1655 to illustrate a mystical treatise called the *Piedra Gloriosa* written by his friend Menasseh Ben Israel. It represents the image seen by Nebuchadnezzar (fig. 27). Rembrandt's intense sympathy with everything alive meant that he could not help drawing statues as if they were real people; all the same, we feel that he might have done something a little more dignified and worshipful than this insecure young man. It is as if the very word image, with all its pompous, official associations had aroused in him a perverse desire to make the figure as underdeveloped and plebeian as possible.

Fig. 27. Rembrandt.
The Image seen by Nebuchadnezzar. [Etching]

Lest it be thought unfair to quote such a small and exceptional work, I will take as my second example a masterpiece of his maturity, the Saul and David in the Mauritshuis (fig. 28). Rembrandt seldom painted a more dramatic figure than the Saul. The head bowed under the weight of its magnificent turban, the single, desperate eye,[18] which warns us that

34

Fig. 28. Rembrandt. Saul and David

another bout of madness is approaching, the nervous, kingly hand on the javelin: no one can fail to be moved by these magnificent inventions. But the harping David is a different matter. The Bible tells us that the young David was "ruddy and withal of a beautiful countenance"; and throughout the whole of Christian art, painters and sculptors had made this the pretext for inventing types of youthful beauty, blond, healthy, curly-haired and heroic. But Rembrandt had never seen a youth of this kind produce enchanting music. On the other hand he had seen, as we all have seen, a young Jewish boy totally absorbed in his art, and had felt that this was the medium through which music could work its magic. Since the mysterious power of music was the subject of his picture, he has disregarded traditional imagery; and the longer one contemplates this picture, the more one admires his imaginative insight. But to the academic eye his David is a painful anachronism; and I will confess that forty years ago, when I first saw the Saul and David in The Hague, I found the figure disturbing.

Rembrandt's refusal to compromise with classic imagery lasted all his life, and this meant that certain subjects in which classic form had, so to say, staked out too strong a claim remained outside his range. He felt convinced, for example, that our first parents could not have been the graceful well-nourished Adam and Eve of Raphael; he conceives them (fig. 29) as un-evolved types of singularly little charm.[19] But this did not satisfy him, and he did not return to the subject again. Although he could draw a lion or an elephant with unequalled skill he was reluctant to draw a horse, because he felt that its rounded quarters had become a cliché of academism. When he has to represent one he either makes it lumpy and

Fig. 29. Rembrandt. Adam and Eve. [Etching]

plebeian, as in the Good Samaritan, or a sort of rocking horse, as in the huge equestrian portrait from Panshanger now in the National Gallery, London. The most anti-classical of all Rembrandt's horses is the emaciated animal in that masterpiece of romantic painting known as the Polish Rider (fig. 30). This horse seems to have evolved from one of those mysterious conjunctions in Rembrandt's mind of which several other examples will

36

Fig. 30. Rembrandt. The Polish Rider

be found in the pages that follow. From his youth onwards he must have known the figure of a skeleton horse and rider which stood high up on the balustrade of the anatomical theatre in Leyden.[20] Its macabre authority fascinated him and at some point[21] he made a brilliant drawing of it (fig. 31). Death on a horse: and Rembrandt, whose imagination was often stirred by the coincidence of names and titles, was reminded of the Four Horsemen in Dürer's Apocalypse (fig. 32) where Death is riding one of the few broken-down horses in western art. Thus he arrived at a horse with the hind legs and quarters of the skeleton, the forelegs of the Dürer, and a head painted from nature with a sense of structure worthy of the Parthenon and a pathos unknown in fifth-century Greece. Meanwhile a new image has

37

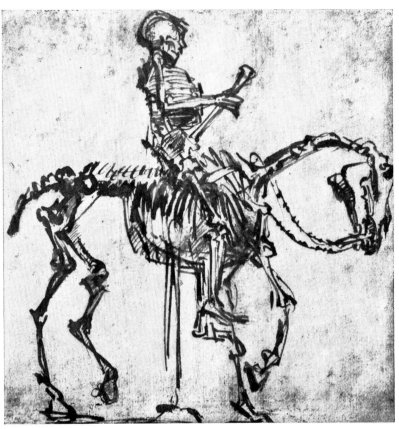

Fig. 31. Rembrandt. Skeleton Rider. [Drawing]

entered his mind, that of the exotic cavalier, probably Hungarian, whose engagements with the Turks played a part in the seventeenth-century imagination. Even the skeleton horseman in Leyden seems to have worn an oriental head-dress and carried a nomadic weapon, a war hammer; they are discernable in the print, although by the time Rembrandt made his drawing they had vanished.[22] So, to Death on a horse is added this concept of a far-ranging Christian knight; and here he may have thought again of Dürer, and of the *Miles Christianus* in the engraving known as the Knight with Death and the Devil, and remembered how the landscape rises oppressively behind the figures. But in contrast to Dürer's heavily armoured knight, grimly resolute on his powerful horse, Rembrandt's rider, on his thin, light-foot nag, wears a elegant *joupane*, and turns towards us, or rather, towards the evening light, a face of almost feminine beauty.[23] He

38

Fig. 32. Dürer. The Four Horsemen of the Apocalypse. [Woodcut]

thus creates one of those antimonies, not infrequent in Rembrandt's later work, which reach a new level of imaginative truth.

The mysterious poetry of the Polish Rider is inseparable from its anti-classical imagery. If the thin rump of his horse were to be transformed into the full, round quarters of a horse by Rubens, the picture would lose its magic. One prosperous, commonplace curve would break its spell. And like several of Rembrandt's later works—the Jewish Bride, the Prodigal Son—it echoes, in an almost uncanny way, a mediaeval or early Christian motive. Its likeness to the Bamberg rider (fig. 33) must be, in the material sense, a coincidence, due to causes which we are still forced, in all humility, to dismiss. But although some of Rembrandt's greatest paintings seem to derive their vital magic from a clairvoyant sympathy with the gothic past, they owe their air of timeless authority to an underlying knowledge of the classical tradition. Without the rebellious, truth-loving, deep-delving energy of Rembrandt's imagination his classicism would have become academic; without a profound study of classic art his gifts as an illustrator would have left him far short of the summit of European art.

Fig. 33. 13th Century. The *Miles Christianus* at Bamberg

40

2

Rembrandt and the High Renaissance

In the first chapter I tried to show how Rembrandt's love of humanity and hatred of shams, mixed with an explosive vitality, made him rebel against the conventional academism of his day, both in its baroque and its classical manifestation. The movement, turbulence and dramatic lighting of Baroque he enjoyed and mastered, but its rhetoric and reliance on emotional clichés he could never swallow. On the contrary, he found in the simplicity and concentration of pre-mannerist art a basis of design which would enable him to present the truth with greater directness. His passion for truth was inseparable from his desire to construct compositions which should have a firm, timeless quality, capable of realisation on a large scale. Just as Keats felt that he could attain true grandeur only by looking past the elegant, sentimental poetry of his time to Milton, Shakespeare, and Homer, so Rembrandt looked back to Leonardo da Vinci and Raphael.

He never went to Italy. The fact that he and Lievens were unwilling to do so is noted with disfavour by Constantin Huygens, and he also records their reason: that in the flower of youth they could not spare time for an Italian journey, and that in any case by staying at home they could see all the Italian art they wanted concentrated in one place, whereas in Italy they would be at pains to visit widely separated places. This famous answer is not entirely convincing, as Huygens had expressly urged them to see paintings of Raphael and Michelangelo, which were concentrated in Rome; but it remains true that an almost incredible quantity of Italian art was to be seen in Amsterdam. We tend to forget that in the seventeenth century there were no public galleries and most of the great private collections were inaccessible. The only places where old masters could be seen and studied at close quarters were the auction rooms.

In 1630 Amsterdam was the centre of the art trade of the world. Collections were sent there to be sold from all over Europe, in particular from Italy. Many Dutch painters were also art dealers—Vermeer, for example, seems to have had no other form of livelihood. Rembrandt was in the thick of the profession. Even before going to Amsterdam he had formed a business connection with the dealer Hendrik van Uylenburgh, and when he moved there he lived in van Uylenburgh's house.[1] Two years later he married van Uylenburgh's cousin, Saskia. He was on close terms with the dealer Pieter de la Tombe, and owned several pictures jointly with him, including a large picture of Christ and the Woman of Samaria attributed to Giorgione. Later in life he chose as guardian for his daughter Cornelia an antiquarian named Abraham Francen; he has left us a portrait of him, one of those rather unattractive, over-finished etchings which he did to please his friends (fig. 34). It shows Francen inspecting a purchase in a typical antiquarian's parlour—thick table-cloth, Limoges enamel triptych and Ming figure—just such a one as might have been found in Amsterdam or Vienna up to the 1930 depression. Rembrandt himself occasionally did a little dealing; he bought and sold a Rubens painting of Hero and Leander, now in Dresden. But principally he was a collector; and contemporaries were agreed that no collector was ever more eager and extravagant. Baldinucci tells us that when he attended an auction where paintings and drawings by great men were offered for sale, he bid so high at the outset that no one else came forward to bid. "He said he did this," says Baldinucci, "*per mettere in credito il professione*," and anyone who has seen pictures at an auctioneer's being thumbed and spat on by prospective purchasers, will sympathise with him. But of course the real reason for these extravagant bids was that certain works of art were absolutely necessary to him. He needed to possess them not simply to enjoy them, but to learn from them.

We are no longer accustomed to the notion that an artist collects in order to instruct himself. The modern artist is glutted, and sometimes choked, by aesthetic experience. He can see hundreds of exhibitions, dozens of picture galleries; and, in photographic reproduction, the whole

42

Fig. 34. Rembrandt. Portrait of Abraham Francen. [Etching]

range of art is available to him. But in the past, artists treated their collections as a poet like Petrarch treated his library, as a source of ideas, technique, and style. Nearly all the leading artists of the seventeenth century were collectors; and none of them, not even Sir Peter Lely, amassed so vast and heterogeneous a collection as Rembrandt. We know a good deal about its contents. As a result of sublime carelessness in money matters he was threatened with bankruptcy, and averted the catastrophe only by what was called a *cessio bonorum:* in other words, he was sold up. The inventory of the sale still exists.[2] It is dated 26th July, 1656, and contains 363 lots. Not all of them are what we would call works of art. There are quantities of marine specimens, shells and coral, such as we see in contemporary Dutch still life paintings; and there is a large collection of ancient and exotic weapons—about a hundred and twenty in the small studio alone, sold in lots of sixty and thirty. The inventory even lists Rem-

43

brandt's own clothes, including three shirts and six handkerchiefs which were at the wash, but surprisingly enough it omits the furs, brocades, and precious stuffs which so much impressed visitors to Rembrandt's house, and which we know so well from his pictures. Probably they had been exempted as the property of Hendrijcke and her daughter Cornelia. Of the paintings, the majority were by contemporaries: Adrian Brouwer and Hercules Seghers, both of whom influenced him, his old master Lastman, his fellow pupil Lievens, and others who have passed into obscurity. There were also works of Italians of the preceding generation, and two copies of Carracci (nos. 81 and 83)[3]; and from these, too, he derived motives and compositions. But his real quarry was the series of *Kunstboecken*, scrapbooks of drawings and engravings, which appear in the inventory of the *Kunst Caemer*, together with his famous collection of antique busts; and it is from these above all that he derived his remarkable knowledge of high renaissance design.

It is ironical that Sandrart, in the disparaging criticism of Rembrandt quoted earlier, should have accused him of neglecting Raphael's "judicious pictorial disposition"; because all his life Rembrandt was a passionate student of Raphael, and it was precisely Raphael's "judicious pictorial disposition" which he made the basis of his mature style. He owned two paintings by Raphael (nos. 67 and 114) and the inventory lists (nos. 196, 205, 214) three large volumes of prints after his works, described as very fine impressions. The value he placed on these may be deduced from a single example: the finest existing impression of the Hundred Guilder Print has a note on the back by a collector named Zoomer saying that he had received it from Rembrandt in exchange for a print of Marcantonio's Plague in Phrygia, and Zoomer makes it clear that he thought he had had the better of the bargain.[4] But having acquired his Marcantonio so extravagantly, Rembrandt seems to have made no direct use of it. As with the greater part of his collection, he let it settle in the back of his mind to build up the great deposit of knowledge on which his style was formed. Occasionally, however, some pose or gesture fulfilled so precisely the needs of his creative imagination that he used it in recognisable form. In his earliest successful picture of a New Testament subject, the Presentation in the Temple, now in Hamburg (fig. 35), the figure of the prophetess Anna is clearly derived from the St. Anne in Marcantonio's

44

Fig. 35. Rembrandt. Presentation in the Temple

Fig. 36. Marcantonio, after Raphael.
The Virgin and Child with St. Anne. [Engraving]

engraving of a beautiful Raphael design (fig. 36). Even so, it is not a quotation, but is completely absorbed into its new context, and is studied afresh from nature, with Rembrandt's mother as the model. He also changes the meaning of the original pose. In the Raphael the raised hands of St. Anne are not merely a gesture of recognition, but imply protection and involuntary benediction. It is a profoundly Catholic gesture which recalls, and was intended to recall, the celebration of the Mass. In the Rembrandt the raised hands of the prophetess Anna are intended to express in an arresting manner her feelings of astonishment; and yet they retain from the earlier usage some accent of divine afflatus which a more naturalistic expression of surprise would have lacked.

As Rembrandt's style evolved, the interaction between motives derived from art and sketches done from life became so close that there often seems to be no division between them. Just as he did not distinguish be-

46

tween episodes in biblical history and scenes in the life around him, so he passes imperceptibly from a remembered motive to a direct notation. This dialogue between art and life may be studied in two drawings of women and children, one in Dresden, the other in the Speelman Collection. The former (fig. 37) is an obvious reminiscence of Raphael's *Madonna della Sedia*. The rhythm of the pose, the turbaned head, even the fringed back of the chair remind us so vividly of the Raphael that for a moment we hardly notice that Rembrandt has left out the child. The other drawing (fig. 38), although in precisely the same style, has all the appearance of a direct notation, and probably was drawn from life, in so far as this is true of any fugitive pose. But Rembrandt's mind was still occupied by the *Madonna della Sedia*, and so the child, omitted in his direct reminiscence, reappeared unconsciously in a sketch of a thing seen.

Fig. 37. Rembrandt.
Sketch, after Raphael's *Madonna della Sedia*

Fig. 38. Rembrandt. Studies from life
[Drawing]

This is, perhaps, the point at which to say something about the study and criticism of Rembrandt's drawings, which must play so great a part in any attempt to follow the workings of his mind. Already in the seventeenth century, de Piles, who owned over three hundred drawings by Rembrandt,

Fig. 39. Bol. The Finding of Moses. [Drawing]

spoke of them as his *pensées*; and they are in fact precious, intimate thoughts on every subject. To attribute to Rembrandt a thought which is not his is to alter his character, sometimes quite considerably; and even to misdate the thought is to misunderstand his development. The extremely personal quality of Rembrandt's drawings makes questions of authenticity far more urgent than in the case of Raphael or even Michelangelo, where the idea is more important than the execution. But, paradoxically enough, the connoisseurship of Rembrandt's drawings is an even more difficult task. In my experience no Italian drawings, not even those of Raphael, present so many insoluble problems. The reason is that for almost thirty years Rembrandt's house was full of pupils to whom he gave personal instruction every day, and whose drawings he corrected. As a teacher he was generous, conscientious, and inspiring to the point of hypnotism. Many of the pupils, Carel Fabritius, Bol, Flinck, Nicholas Maes, Philip de Koninck and Aert de Gelder, were artists of considerable skill and distinc-

Fig. 40. School of Raphael. The Finding of Moses. [Pen, bistre and wash]

tion; and under his eye even secondary painters like Drost and van der Pluym were capable of excellent work. The critical study of Rembrandt drawings is still in a fluid state. A very high percentage of those reproduced in Valentiner's two volumes would not now be accepted by any serious scholar; and of the fifteen hundred drawings published as authentic in Dr. Benesch's great corpus, Professor Rosenberg[5] has questioned (in my opinion correctly) the attribution of at least fifty. Equally about thirty of the drawings rejected by Benesch seem to me authentic. Practically none of the usual criteria of connoisseurship is valid. For example, those elements in a work of art which Morelli relied on for proof, hands, draperies, and other details which are supposed to reveal the unconscious mental patterns of an artist, seem to have been precisely what Rembrandt's pupils could reproduce most accurately. Nor is his calligraphy, in my experience, a safe guide, for his pupils were able to imitate his loops and flourishes with extraordinary assurance. Weaknesses of structure are more revealing, for there is usually evidence of knowledge behind Rembrandt's hastiest scribble: but certain etchings of unquestionable authenticity, like the portrait of himself and Saskia of 1636, contain weaknesses which, if they occurred in a drawing, would lead us to condemn it.[6] On the whole I have found that the pupils break down at precisely that point where Rembrandt's unique natural gift first asserted itself—facial expression. Their heads tend to be formalistic and typical, whereas Rembrandt, in the smallest jotting, is able to endow his faces with intense individual life. But this is not an infallible rule; and in the last resort I fear that our judgement of the authenticity of a Rembrandt drawing is a subjective matter depending largely on aesthetic responses. Needless to say, close daily intimacy with the whole range of his work is also necessary.

I have inserted this parenthesis at this point because it happens that several of the drawings which show most clearly Rembrandt's debt to Italian art are of questionable authenticity. Indeed if such a drawing is too close to its original it is automatically suspect, for as a rule Rembrandt altered a motive to his own needs and nearly always changed the subject. Perhaps for this reason the reminiscence of the *Madonna della Sedia* does not appear in Dr. Benesch's corpus, although personally I am convinced that it is authentic. An example of the same problems where I take the opposite view is a graceful drawing of the Finding of Moses now in the Rijksmuseum (fig. 39). In grouping and movement it is obviously related to Raphael's design on the ceiling of the Loggia, and two of the figures recall those in preparatory sketches by Raphael's pupil, Giovanni Penni (fig. 40). That Rembrandt should have followed them so closely in treating the same subject is improbable, and leads us to examine the drawing more critically. The longer we do so, the more it becomes evident that the loops and flourishes are purely calligraphic and have no underlying sense of structure. It is almost a relief to find that the drawing corresponds to a painting by Bol in the Hague, and comparison with Bol's known drawings shows that he specialised in a free and fanciful calligraphy, much at variance with his pedestrian style as a painter.[7]

In contrast to such easily recognisable borrowings we shall see again and again Rembrandt absorbing a motive so completely that we should be in doubt if there really were any direct connection with the earlier

50

Fig. 41. Rembrandt. The Blindness of Tobit. [Etching]

prototype, could we not, in several instances, follow the process step by
step. An example is the etching of the Blindness of Tobit (fig. 41). This
seems to be one of Rembrandt's most touchingly natural figures, and our
first impulse is to say that it must have been done directly from experience.
We then remember the Elymas struck with blindness, in Raphael's cartoon, which was certainly known to Rembrandt through Agostino Vene-

ziano's engraving (fig. 42). Out of all the conceivable ways of representing blindness, are not the similarities of rhythm and pose almost too great for coincidence? And is not the unforgettable simplicity of Rembrandt's Tobit—the quintessence of blindness— an indication of some deeply secreted experience, rather than mere observation? The more we study Rembrandt, the more we are inclined to answer yes to both these questions. From the first he had an incredibly retentive visual memory, and this applied to works of art as well as to transient impressions of movement or gesture. We can even say that his memories of works of art were always present in his mind like rough moulds into which he could pour his immediate sensations. This is the classic procedure, recommended in academies; but just as the cones and cylinders of academic instruction were transformed by the violence of Cézanne's "*petites sensations*," so Rembrandt's intense participation in human emotions allowed him to use traditional moulds with no sense of constriction or hackneyed precedent.

Fig. 42. Agostino Veneziano after Raphael.
The Blinding of Elymas (detail). [Engraving]

Fig. 43. Rembrandt. Copy of Leonardo da Vinci's Last Supper. [Red chalk]

How far was Rembrandt's memory of the motives and designs of earlier artists fortified by actual copying? We are led to ask this question because of one work, which we know had a profound influence on him, Leonardo da Vinci's Last Supper, several of his copies have survived. The earliest evidence of his interest in this pivotal design is the under-drawing of a famous sheet now in the Lehman Collection (formerly Dresden; fig. 43). It is done with a hard pinkish chalk, which has now grown faint, and is largely obscured by the bold red chalk outlines which Rembrandt himself added later. This under-drawing is, clearly perceptible in the Christ's head and hand, the apostles immediately to His right and the dog in the right hand corner. The dog, which does not appear in any other version of

53

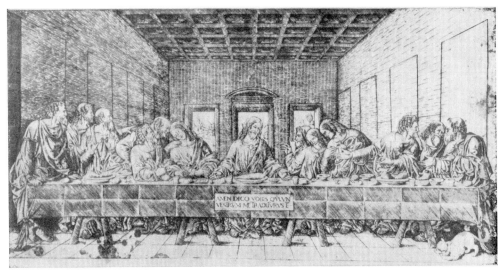

Fig. 44. Milanese Sixteenth Century. The Last Supper, after Leonardo da Vinci. [Engraving]

Leonardo's Last Supper, proves that Rembrandt was following an early sixteenth century Milanese engraving by the master of the Sforza Book of Hours (fig. 44). Although this is the earliest reproduction of the Cenacolo which has come down to us, it gives a very feeble notion of the power of the original, and Rembrandt has made of it a somewhat niggling copy; but when he went over it again with a softer chalk he used the free vigorous strokes with which he corrected his pupils' drawings. The boldness and angularity of the strokes has led scholars to suggest that they were added much later; but they are in the same style as some copies of Lastman which he made in the mid '30's, and need not be more than a year or two later than the timid under-drawing. What made him go over his old drawing in this high-handed manner? It was the sight or acquisition of a more faithful copy of the Last Supper.[8] The proof of this lies in the figure of Judas. In the engraving he is almost upright and the diagonal line of his arm is lost. But it was precisely this diagonal, this powerful recoil, which had most interest for Leonardo, especially in conjunction with the thrust-forward, elongated cranium of St. Peter. The moment Rembrandt saw it, he recognised its dramatic and symbolic importance, and made it the strongest accent in his reworking of the group; and his other alterations argue the vivid impact of some copy far closer to Leonardo's original.

54

Fig. 45. Rembrandt. Copy of Leonardo da Vinci's Last Supper (fragment). [Drawing]

If, as I believe, the reworking was done about 1635, this was the moment when Rembrandt was most anxious to master the principles of baroque design. He has therefore disregarded the severe classic symmetry of Leonardo's setting, and introduced instead an asymmetrical canopy; and in a second drawing, of which only a fragment remains (fig. 45), he has treated the group with greater freedom, although he has given the heads of Judas and St. Peter their correct relationship, as in the fresco and not the engraving. Finally (fig. 46), he sees if he can turn Leonardo's balanced group

Fig. 46. Rembrandt. Free copy of Leonardo da Vinci's Last Supper. [Pen and ink]

55

Fig. 47. Rembrandt. Samson's Wedding Feast

into the kind of baroque free-for-all which was occupying his creative energies in the 1630's. The figures, grouped around the off-centre figure of Christ, surge and sway with unclassical abandon. The man leaning forward to the left and the man clasping his hands are pure Rembrandt. The powerful motive of St. Matthew pointing one way with both his hands, and looking the other, is abandoned, and a typical Rembrandtesque rabbi figure heaves his whole body towards the end of the table. Only the recoiling Judas and St. Peter retain their original character. Evidently Rembrandt attached some importance to this copy, for not only is it on squared paper, but it is signed, and dated 1635.

But although, in this drawing, Rembrandt has departed so far from the original design of the Cenacolo, the power of Leonardo's composition still weighed heavily on him, so heavily that all his life he never again drew, painted, or etched the Last Supper. That the greatest illustrator of the Christian story since Giotto should have omitted this central episode,

56

Fig. 48. Rembrandt. Christ Healing the Sick. [Etching]

shows how Rembrandt avoided subjects (the Annunciation is another example) in which the formal possibilities were exhausted. In the course of his life the experience of Leonardo's Last Supper took many forms. In 1638 there was the baroque response, outcome of the drawing of 1635, the sumptuous picture at Dresden of Samson asking riddles at his wedding feast (fig. 47). The transformation of Leonardo's Christ into this sly, watchful, well-fed bride may seem slightly sacrilegious; and perhaps Rembrandt himself was barely conscious of the source of the composition. Indeed when we compare it with the Last Supper, the two groups have little enough in common: yet the isolation of that pale, triangular central figure cannot be independent of Leonardo's first inspiration. A few years later the Last Supper is still in his mind when collecting material for his baroque masterpiece, the Hundred Guilder Print (fig. 48), and provides a curious illustration of his mental economy. The figure of St. Matthew, who was cut out of the Last Supper drawing of 1635, the man with the head turned

57

Fig. 49. Rembrandt. Study for Christ Healing the Sick. [Drawing]

Fig. 50. Rembrandt. Detail of Christ Healing the Sick. [Etching]

58

Fig. 51. Rembrandt. The Supper at Emmaus

one way and two arms pointing another, reappears as a leading figure in
the crowd of sick people and their relatives. He is most easily identified in
one of the few drawings for the etching (fig. 49); in the etching itself he is
reduced to a less prominent position, but is still recognisably a classic
figure, the admixture of realism bringing him closer to Masaccio than to
Leonardo. The group of skeptical Pharisees on the left is also a reminiscence of Leonardo's apostles (fig. 50), including the Judas and the man

59

with the upward pointing hand, who appears in the first copy of the engraving, and was not redrawn.[9]

More important is Rembrandt's use of that figure which since it was invented has haunted the European imagination, Leonardo's Christ. Since he cannot bring himself to attempt a Last Supper, he adapts the figure to the subject of the Supper at Emmaus. This subject had inspired one of his most brilliant early paintings, the panel in the Jacquemart André Museum; but in 1648 these dramatic triumphs were abandoned for a far more profound interpretation—"as he sat at meat with them he took bread, and blessed it, and brake it, and gave to them; and their eyes were opened, and they knew him". So the picture in the Louvre of 1648 (fig. 51), at once the most touching and the most classical work of Rembrandt's middle period, is related to the Last Supper by subject as well as design. In this case, however, there was an intermediary, Dürer's woodcut in the Small Passion of 1511. The Christ breaking bread, and the attitudes of the two apostles, leave us in no doubt that it was Dürer who suggested to Rembrandt how Leonardo's motive could be transferred from the institution of the

Fig. 52. Rembrandt. Christ Appearing to the Apostles. [Pen and ink]

Fig. 53. Rembrandt. The Syndics

Eucharist to its earliest confirmation.[10] A later variation on the theme
of Leonardo's Last Supper is a drawing of Christ appearing to the
Apostles (fig. 52), which must date from the middle 1650's. As in a late
quartet by Beethoven the phrases have become detached and separated,
yet they beckon to each other across the intervening spaces by means of
their emotional power; and we can still recognise the symbols which had
impressed him most forcibly, the open, vulnerable, sacrificial pose of
Christ, and the recoiling diagonal of Judas.

Such are a few of the subjects in which Rembrandt's study of Leonardo's Last Supper consciously influenced his design. But the lessons he
learnt from it were at the back of his mind on many more occasions. Two
of the greatest of his later works, the Conspiracy of Claudius Civilis (fig. 88)
and the Syndics (fig. 53), would surely have been rather different if Leonardo had never worked out his great formal equation; and I do not say

61

Fig. 54. Rembrandt. Study of a "Syndic". [Pen and wash]

this simply because the Syndics are a group of men sitting behind a table. Take the figure of the bearded elderly *staalmeester* second from the left. Had he been seated the group would have become monotonous. Had he been standing, as he was when Rembrandt drew him (fig 54.), he would have held up the flow of movement through the group. Rembrandt has given

Fig. 55. Rembrandt. Girl at a Window

him the difficult and unusual pose of a man rising to his feet; unusual,
that is to say, before the time of Leonardo's Last Supper, where it is the
visible expression of horrified surprise ("one of you will betray me") and
the mainspring of the whole design. In fact Rembrandt has remembered
the figure of St. Bartholomew on the extreme left, who is emphasised in
all his copies.

This close study of Leonardo's Last Supper leads us to speculate as to whether or not Rembrandt could have known Leonardo's famous treatise on painting. On two counts the *Trattato* would have confirmed his own deepest beliefs, first in the stress it lays on gesture and movement as a means of expressing the emotions; and secondly in its repeated references to the beauty of shadows, night scenes and darkness. Thirty years ago, in writing of Leonardo, I twice compared his descriptions of paintable subjects with pictures by Rembrandt, and I cannot improve on the examples I quoted then. "Very great charm of shadow and light," says Leonardo, "is to be found in the faces of those who sit in the doors of dark houses. The eye of the spectator sees that the part of the face which is lit draws its brilliancy from the splendour of the sky. From this intensification of light and shade the face gains greatly in relief .... and in beauty."[11] With the Mona Lisa and the St. Anne in mind we can just conceivably see this as a Leonardo subject. But how much more readily do we associate it with such works by Rembrandt as the Girl at a Window at Chicago (fig. 55) or the Girl Leaning on a Sill at Dulwich! My other example is one of several passages in the *Trattato* describing how to paint a night piece:

"The figures which are seen against the fire look dark in the glare of the firelight; and those who stand at the side are half dark and half red, while those who are visible beyond the edges of the flames will be feebly lighted by the ruddy glow against a black background. As to their gestures, make those which are near it screen themselves with their hands and cloaks, to ward off the intense heat, and some with their faces turned away as if drawing back. Of those further off, represent some of them with their hands raised to screen their eyes, hurt by the intolerable splendour of the flames."[12]

Needless to say, nothing in Leonardo's work is in any way related to this description; and even the 'night pieces' of the Venetians (except, perhaps, an occasional Bassano like his altarpiece in San Giorgio Maggiore, Venice) were less circumstantial. But a number of Rembrandt's pictures, for example the Adoration (fig. 56), come near to illustrating it, nearer even than Honthorst and the other *tenebristi*. Taken by themselves, however, these coincidences of subject, do not prove that Rembrandt had read the *Trattato*. In order to establish this it must be shown, first that the *Trattato* was available to him, and, secondly, that some

64

Fig. 56. Rembrandt. The Adoration of the Shepherds

Fig. 57. Rembrandt. Killing an Ox. [Pen and ink]

Fig. 58. Illustration to Leonardo da Vinci's *Trattato della Pittura*. [ed. 1651]

66

figure in his work was borrowed from an illustrated copy of Leonardo's treatise. The *Trattato* was not printed until 1651, when it appeared together with Alberti's *della Pittura* and, although there is reason to believe that Rembrandt owned this volume of Leonardo's writings, if the *Trattato* had had an influence on his work at a formative period he must have had access to it earlier than this. In fact we know that a manuscript of the *Trattato* was in Amsterdam from 1637 to 1641, in the possession of no less a person than Sandrart. It was one of the copies with illustrative diagrams made under the direction of Nicolas Poussin.[13] Although Sandrart in his *Academie* glosses over the fact that he knew Rembrandt (a vulgar, bankrupt fellow would not have been a suitable friend to this ornament of the profession), there is plenty of evidence that they did know each other, and we can properly suppose that Rembrandt, the determined self-educator, would have importuned him for a sight of a book which Carracci said would have spared him twenty years of labour. The actual text was likely to be more sympathetic to him than Poussin's rather formalised diagrams. However, one group of Rembrandt's drawings shows what is almost certainly a reminiscence of a design in the *Trattato*. The first of these is a drawing in Munich of a man killing an ox, of which the biblical and legendary significance is uncertain (fig. 57).[14] Rembrandt would certainly have known engravings of Raphael's Sacrifice at Lystra; it is therefore all the more significant that he has rejected the Raphael ox-slayer in favour of a pose which occurs as the heading of Chapter XXXIII of the *Trattato, del movimento dell'huomo*. (I reproduce the engraving from the printed version: fig. 58.) As usual he has tried to adapt an academic pose to a real action, and in doing so has got into trouble with the left leg, which in Poussin's figures is a purely classical conception, that invention of Greek art which I have elsewhere called the heroic diagonal. Rembrandt has gone over it several times, and finally lost it altogether. Although its learned artificiality was foreign to him, Rembrandt was determined to use this pose in a definitive work; and we can watch him assimilating it in two drawings of an executioner and a kneeling figure, in Turin, (Val. 280) and in the British Museum (fig. 59), which are studies for the etching of the beheading of John the Baptist (fig. 60). The date on the etching, 1640, tells us when he was studying Leonardo's *Trattato*. It happens that two other direct quotations from Leonardo belong to the same period.

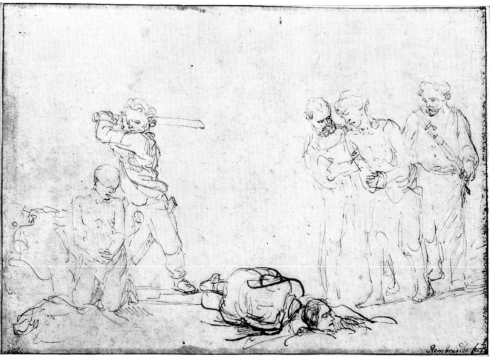

Fig. 59. Rembrandt (? copy), Beheading of Prisoners. [Pen and ink]

Fig. 60. Rembrandt. Beheading of the Baptist. [Etching]

68

Fig. 61. Rembrandt. Joseph & his Brethren. [Pen and ink]

These are the two heads of old men which appear on the left of a drawing of Joseph and his brethren in Amsterdam (fig. 61), datable about 1642. They are obviously derived from those grotesque profiles by Leonardo which seem to us the least attractive of his drawings, but which fascinated pre-humanitarian connoisseurs. Books of engravings of such profiles were published by Hollar in 1645 and by Sandrart in 1654, but Rembrandt's drawing antedates these publications, and by its touch it shows signs of having been imitated from an original Leonardo. In fact the Arundel Leonardos, of which a majority are now at Windsor, were probably in Amsterdam at this date, although it is doubtful if Rembrandt could have had access to them. Needless to say, Rembrandt's eye was not taken by the deformity and monstrosity which made Leonardo's caricatures so attractive to the seventeenth century (Sandrart's publication is actually entitled *Variae Figurae Monstruosae*), but by their intense vitality and eco-

69

Fig. 62. Rembrandt. The Holy Family with a Cat

nomy of line. Having once studied and reproduced them, he never let them appear again in his work.[15] They had been completely absorbed.

The phase of Rembrandt's art that led him to turn the classic symmetry of the Last Supper into the baroque turbulence of Samson's Wedding, lasted until the painting of the Night Watch in 1642 (fig. 78). As with the Blinding of Samson, this huge canvas was a climax preceding a change of style. Although basically not a baroque design (see p. 85) it helped him to get the bustle and elaborations of Baroque out of his system. True, he continued to work on another great masterpiece in that style, the Hundred Guilder Print. But from 1645 to 1650 his compositions became simpler and more tranquil. Pictures like the Holy Family at Cassel (fig. 62) have an air of naturalness and domestic poetry that involves less conspicuous art. Rembrandt, we feel, is anxious to tell the truth; but in all the arts, truth is at the mercy of style: an image must not only be true, but seem true in the showing. So Rembrandt, in order to speak naturally in a consistent and memorable manner had to master new prin-

Fig. 63. Rembrandt. Portrait of Saskia

ciples of design. In the first place he began to study compositions in which the figures are placed parallel with the picture plane, as in a frieze or relief. With the advantage of hindsight we may observe that once or twice Rembrandt had made unexpected use of such parallel compositions, even at a date when he was plunging most exuberantly into depth. An example is a portrait of Saskia (fig. 63) at Cassel, where the profile pose recalls Leonardo's famous drawing of Isabella d'Este, to which has been added, in the hat and collar, a reminiscence of some decorative gothic portraitist, perhaps Cranach, whose woodcuts he had collected (inv. no. 208). But after 1650 Rembrandt made a careful study of relief composition. A drawing of the Entombment (fig. 64) in the Teyler Museum, Haarlem, is an example of how he taught himself. It is a copy of a renaissance design known to us in two contemporary Italian copies, one in the Fogg Museum, Cambridge, Mass. (fig. 65) and the other in the Louvre. We may for convenience refer to it as a Polidoro da Caravaggio.[16] The version used by Rembrandt contained some features that appear in one drawing, some in another—for example the man on the left, with his hands on his head, follows the Louvre drawing, whereas the man on the right is closer to the Fogg drawing. Clearly Rembrandt owned a third version, which may have been the original. Of course he has made many small modifications. He has replaced the conventional draperies of classicism with simple dateless dress, and thereby seems to have transported the figures back from the High Renaissance into the Quattrocento. The mourner on the left now suggests Bellini rather than Raphael. The smooth transitions are replaced by definite intervals; Rembrandt has slightly increased the depth of the relief, making deep pools where there had only been shallows. But as a whole he has preserved, and even clarified, the essentials of the design with extraordinary sureness. This is the kind of classic exercise that preceded some of his noblest compositions. It is interesting to see how little either his pupils or subsequent critics have understood his aims. A drawing in Berlin (fig. 66), obviously based on the same source, is by a pupil whose work occurs fairly frequently in collections of Rembrandt's drawings. The lack of structure in all the figures, the stupid ugly heads and the feeble indication of the Christ's legs, leave me in no doubt that it is not authentic.[17] It is of interest only because it shows that although Rembrandt's pupils could imitate his style, they could not fathom his

72

Fig. 64. Rembrandt. The Entombment, after Polidoro da Caravaggio. [Drawing]

Fig. 65. After Polidoro da Caravaggio. The Entombment. [Drawing]

Fig. 66. Rembrandt pupil. The Entombment. [Drawing]

Fig. 67. Rembrandt. The Entombment. [Drawing]

74

deeper purpose. This vulgarian has thought that the original design, with its severe relief conception, was a bore, and has not only tried to give it a spurious liveliness, but also a spurious depth, by turning round the two figures in the foreground, so that they are in incompetent foreshortening. This is not the way in which Rembrandt transformed his models. He let them grow in his mind until they produced something completely fresh, yet fundamentally related. We know the next phase of this particular idea, a drawing in Berlin (fig. 67) where the arch, the leading figures and the standing men are still distantly reminiscent of Polidoro's drawing; but in the etching of 1658–59 (fig. 68) nothing of the original is left except the high wall, the double arch, and the skulls. It appears to work its effect on our feelings by its rendering of light; its classical origins are hidden; and yet behind its luminous naturalism is a noble solemnity of design, that argues the classical tradition. From 1650 onwards many of Rembrandt's drawings are models of the kind of classicism described by

Fig. 68. Rembrandt. The Entombment by Torchlight.
[Etching]

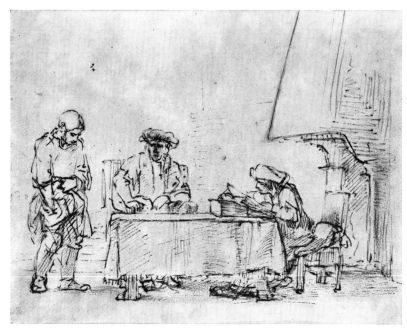

Fig. 69. Rembrandt. The Undutiful Servant. [Drawing]

Wölfflin; that is to say they are clear and economical, free from decorative ornament, dedicated to the episode they depict, and set in a rationally constructed space. Such a drawing as the Undutiful Servant in the Louvre (fig. 69) shows a spareness and concentration comparable with Wölfflin's favourite example of *Klassische Kunst*, Andrea del Sarto's frescoes in the Scalzo.

How far is Rembrandt's classicism in the stylistic sense related to the more general meaning of the word which implies a connection with the art of Greece and Rome? Of course the two can never be disassociated. The restraint and economy of the Greek mind, together with certain technical means of conveying this to the eye, recur in European art at almost every period and are what we mean by the classical tradition. The question is, how far Rembrandt's classicism was absorbed through the Renaissance, and how far he was inspired directly by works of art of Graeco-Roman antiquity.

Professor van Gelder has shown[18] that a surprising quantity of antique sculpture was sold in Holland in the seventeenth century; for example, a collection of "marble statues" was shipped from Antwerp to Amsterdam in 1646 by an intermediary named Michel le Blon. It was divided between twenty-six leading citizens, amongst whom was Rembrandt. His 1656 inventory mentions a number of antiques and casts of antiques, amongst them a series of twenty busts of Roman emperors, that stood in the *Kunst Caemer*, alongside the minerals, the porcelain cups, and the Japanese armour. There were eight other busts of emperors in the back room, a fact which gives some idea of the size of Rembrandt's establishment. It used to be assumed that these were casts, but I think this is incorrect, because when a piece of sculpture is a cast the inventory always lists it as such, "*een pleyster gietsal van een Greeks antiq.*" I believe that these busts were original marbles, and probably included the eighteen emperors which Sir Dudley Carleton had sold to the Netherlands in 1618.[19]

Antique busts do not make the modern auctioneer's heart beat faster. But for over three hundred years, from the time of Mantegna to that of Townley, they were the inspiration of poets and artists and did for the collectors what the so-called impressionists do today: no fashionable collection could be without them. In consequence they were extremely expensive, and we can understand why Saskia's ample dowry was rapidly exhausted. History in the seventeenth century was written in terms of biography, and these busts were valued largely for historical reasons; they were the likenesses of the great actors on the stage of history, whose faces could be compared with their deeds. This, no doubt, was a large part of their interest for Rembrandt in his capacity as an historical painter. But I think he also felt, as other artists have done,[20] the curious *rapport* that exists between sculpture and real people. All the sculpture in his work is disturbingly animated. His drawings of the heads of his Roman emperors (fig. 70) have an almost caricatural effect; the bust in the picture in the Metropolitan Museum known as The Auctioneer seems to be speaking to us behind the sitter's back.

Fig. 70. Rembrandt.
Bust of the Emperor Galba. [Drawing]

But amongst Rembrandt's busts was one that had a deeper meaning for him, the bust of Homer (fig. 71). It touched his imagination, not only because Homer was the father of poetry, but because he was blind. Rembrandt, endowed above all other men, except, perhaps, Leonardo da Vinci, with the power of sight, turned again and again to the theme of blindness: the blindness of Tobit, the blind Isaac blessing Jacob, the blind Homer, who was the subject of one of his latest paintings, now in the Mauritshuis. And in almost all of these the Homer bust is in his mind.

In addition to the busts, the inventory lists a quantity of antique sculpture, including a cast of the Laocoön (no. 329). But Rembrandt's own collection contained only a very small proportion of the antiques in Holland at the time[21], to many of which he must have had access. How far did he study and copy them? The inventory gives an unexpected and decisive answer; it contains one album of drawings of the antique by Rembrandt (no. 251) and another book of statues (no. 261) drawn "from life"—to repeat the Irish-ism of the inventory—*een boeckie vol statuen van Rembrandt na'et leven geteecknet*. None of these drawings of the antique has survived. It would be interesting to know if they were done with the same lack of respect for ideal form as the drawings of the busts, or the image seen by Nebuchadnezzar. Finally there were books of engravings after the antique, probably scrap-books, which were popular in the seventeenth century (two of them, nos. 226–7, are listed in the inventory without titles). Why did Rembrandt spend so much money and time in studying the antique? Other artists did so as a matter of unthinking conformity: belief in the ultimate authority of Graeco-Roman art had entered the academic curriculum in the Renaissance, and had come to be accepted like a religious axiom. But Rembrandt, as we have seen, had no uncritical veneration of antiquity; and when he copied works of art he had a practical end in view. It is easy to see what he was looking for in Raphael or Mantegna; but what could he gain from the posturing marble divinities, smooth, soulless and inane, which were the show pieces of a seventeenth-century collection? What could have induced him to draw them "from life"?

The answer is that Rembrandt, like every other artist who has considered the matter, recognised in these feeble works the paradigm of a fully integrated and harmonious system of forms which could be applied,

78

Fig. 71. Rembrandt. Aristotle Contemplating a Bust of Homer

Fig. 72. Rembrandt. The Angel departing from Tobit (1641). [Etching]

by analogy, to living experience. I cannot say that I have found much direct evidence that he profited by his study of figures in the round; but his study of antique reliefs had a profound effect on his sense of design and even on his imagination. I will give two examples.

Rembrandt's mind was much occupied by the subject of angels. Like Vaughan, he loved to think of the time when they conversed familiarly with men, and moved among them unrecognised; and in his baroque period he was particularly devoted to the moment of their departure, which was the pretext for a sudden illumination and a dramatic movement into depth. It was a baroque subject, and the picture in the Louvre of the Angel Leaving Tobias dated 1637 is one of Rembrandt's most consistent excercises in the baroque style. A few years later, in 1641, he confided the subject to an etching plate (fig. 72). The treatment is less obviously dramatic, and more domestic, the group of figures beautifully and variously involved; but the angel still shows the soles of his rather too rustic feet. Then, for the next twelve years, he continued to brood on the appearances of angels, and came to the same conclusion as the creators of early Christian iconography, that they must have resembled the winged victories on antique monuments. We see the result in a drawing of the Angel Leaving Tobit, datable about 1656, which is like a classical commentary on the

80

Fig. 73. Rembrandt. The Angel departing from Tobit (*c.* 1656). [Drawing]

etching of 1641 (fig. 73). The angel is a spandrel figure from a triumphal arch. In the original he would have been draped, and would have been carrying a torch in his hands; but otherwise his pose and movement are exactly the same. I must confess that I have not yet been able to find out where Rembrandt discovered this particular Victory. The spandrel figures on the arch at Pola are the most like, but I doubt if they had been engraved, and a more probable source would be an incompetent representation of the Arch of Titus. The diagonal movement of this spandrel relief has dictated the design of the family group. They no longer revolve round one another, with numerous changes of axis; Tobit and his son form a severe, inward-turning triangle, geometrically related to the vertical of the door and the horizontal of Tobit's staff; and the diagonal of Tobit's back leads our eye, with almost archaic directness, to the departing angel. Thus Rem-

Fig. 74. Rembrandt. Study of a Nude Model. [Drawing]

brandt has not merely borrowed an image from antique art, but has allowed it to control his whole system of composition.

My other example shows an even more complete and surprising absorption. The Bathsheba in the Louvre (fig. 75) is one of the most intimate and personal of all his works; it is a portrait of Hendrickje (for once we can be sure of this) and was no doubt painted from life. But the finality of the design, and its parallelism with the picture plane, warn us that the pose was not arrived at without study. A large number of life drawings of this date have come down to us, and show, for the most part, a very direct approach to the model. One of these drawings, now in the Louvre (fig. 74), must, I think, have been his first thought for the Bathsheba. It has not hitherto been recognised as such, but the untidy bundle on the left, which already suggests the prostrate figure of Bathsheba's servant (and was later to be promoted to the second plane) seems to make the identification

82

Fig. 75. Rembrandt. Bathsheba

certain. However, the nude figure itself was not compact and stable enough
to be carried out on a large scale, and might have remained no more than
a study, had it not collided, in Rembrandt's imagination, with an engraving of an antique relief (fig. 76). This he found in a book which had

wide circulation in the seventeenth century, François Perrier's *Icones et Segmenta*, published in Paris in 1645.[22] It represents a woman,[23] perhaps a bride, covering her face with her cloak, while a maid bathes her feet. We may surmise that it was her gesture of shame, no less than the solemnity of the whole design, which appealed to Rembrandt, and reminded him of the subject of Bathsheba. Turning the pages of Perrier's book in a mood of creative hunger he found two other engravings which nourished him. One of them showed him how to give the nude torso of his figure more clarity than it had in his study from the model; another showed him an alternative to the hand covering the face—for inevitably the expression on Bathsheba's face was to be of supreme importance to him. From this engraving he took the inclination of the head, and the position of the right arm, which allowed him to add that marvellous stroke of dramatic and pictorial invention, the hand holding the letter from David. As for the other hand, which critics of the last century loved to describe as the broad, peasant hand of Hendrickje, it turns out to be a fairly close reminiscence of the hand in the relief, although no doubt it was painted from nature.

So these crude engravings of third-rate artifacts helped to inspire one of the most beautiful pictures in the world, simply because they could transmit a system of design perfected in the fifth century B C., the great form-determining period of the European mind.

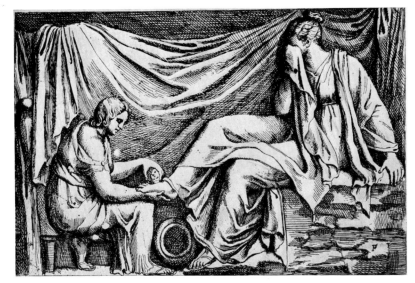

Fig. 76. François Perrier. Antique relief. [Engraving]

84

3

Rembrandt
and the Monumental Tradition

Rembrandt's study of high renaissance design involved a conscious effort to master the science of large scale composition. In addition to engravings of Raphael's madonnas and smaller figure pieces he had undoubtedly seen prints of the tapestry cartoons and of the frescoes in the *stanze*, then considered the summit of art. Rembrandt determined that he would achieve the same eminence. Scholars have tended to suppose that this was an ambition of his later period when he is known to have executed two or three paintings for architectural settings. But in 1642, when he painted his largest surviving picture, the Night Watch (fig. 77), he already had this aim in mind. The Night Watch is conveniently classified as Baroque. Put it beside a work of true Baroque, say Guercino's St. William of Aquitaine, painted some twenty years earlier, and the high renaissance basis of Rembrandt's composition is immediately apparent. Instead of the enormous, twisting, asymmetrical figures of the Bolognese, which, combined with apparitions in the sky, create a feeling of sublime unreality, Rembrandt's figures are firmly established in a given space. They step forward to the centre of the stage from under a grandiose central archway. This arched portico was more obviously Raphaelesque before the picture was cut down,[1] as we can see from a copy in the National Gallery (fig. 78)[2]: and before a baroque cartouche with the names of the company was added, some time after Rembrandt's death. This copy also shows more clearly the perspective scheme, with a central vanishing point and a balanced disposition of the figures, established by a slight diagonal movement from the right to the centre, an effect lost when more than a seventh was cut from the left-hand side of the original canvas. This is the

Fig. 77. Rembrandt. The Night Watch

type of composition which was brought to perfection by Raphael in the Vatican, and we know from many examples that Rembrandt looked at engravings of the *stanze* throughout his life. In the Night Watch the proportion of the figures to the surrounding space is that of the *Stanza d'Eliodoro* (i.e., considerably larger than in the *Stanza della Segnatura*), and we know that from these frescoes he had not only borrowed individual figures, but also studied the complete compositions, for there exists a fragment of a drawing after the Repulse of Attila,[3] which has been attributed to Rembrandt and is certainly in his style. In the Night Watch the animated central group, knotted together by a piece of foreshortening, the man in armour raised on the left (Pope Leo in the Attila), the excited coming and going of subsidiary figures in the second plane, and the static frontal portraits in the background, are all part of Raphael's machinery of picture-

86

Fig. 78. After Rembrandt. The Night Watch

making, and look Baroque only because they are garnished by Rembrandt's rich accoutrements and dramatic lighting. In fact, it was this high renaissance scale, proportion and construction, quite as much as chiaroscuro, which distinguished the Night Watch from the other Dutch group portraits of the seventeenth century. They were of oblong, sometimes even panoramic form, in order that all the members should be in the front row, whereas Rembrandt decided on the classic proportion of 3×4, and thereby opened the way to difficulties of *placement* which were long thought to have brought him into disfavour, and certainly gave trouble to the company's leader, Captain Frans Banning Cocq. We must add that although his pink, inarticulate face does not suggest a high degree of intelligence, Captain Cocq remained proud of his act of patronage, and had a copy of his Sortie made for his family album. In 1715 the vast canvas was transferred to the Town Hall of Amsterdam, where it was hung

87

Fig. 79. Rembrandt. Christ Presented to the People (1655).
[Etching, 1st state]

in the War Council Chamber; so that, in a sense, Rembrandt's ambition to have a heroic work of renaissance proportions decorating a public building was ultimately achieved.

Although the old legend of dissatisfaction with the Night Watch is now discredited, it remains true that soon after it was painted fashionable taste veered away from Rembrandt. The very pupils whom he himself had trained, Dou, Flinck, Bol, were preferred to him, partly because they maintained a higher polish, partly because their work seemed to have a more international flavour. Fashion has so strong a grip on culvitated society—is, indeed, with good manners, part of the cement which holds society together—that figures on the social stage cannot afford to see past it to what is fundamental in the art of their time. When, about the year 1650, Constantin Huygens was advising the widow of Prince Frederick Henry[4] on the decoration of the Huis ten Bosch, her country palace near The Hague, he did not recommend the employment of the artist whom twenty years earlier he had praised so extravagantly; and the commissions went to Soutman, van Everdingen and Bol.

88

Fig. 80. Lucas van Leyden. Christ Presented to the People. (1510) [Engraving]

One cannot but suppose that Rembrandt was deeply disappointed, for it was precisely at this time that he felt most interest in historical and religious subjects involving complex groups of figures; and he knew himself to be capable of carrying them out on a large scale. We can tell this from the grandiose compositional schemes which appear in his drawings and etchings. One of these, the etching of Christ Presented to the People (fig. 79), I have mentioned already to illustrate his change from a curvilinear to a rectilinear style. It is the most severe and authoritarian of all his designs. The basic idea is a contrast between frontal, implacable architecture, symbolising the rule of abstract justice, and swarming, disordered humanity; with the accompanying theme of Christ and the high priest being presented on a higher plane, and, as it were, more rigidly encased in their abstract setting. No doubt Rembrandt's first thoughts on the subject were influenced by an engraving (B.71) by Lucas van Leyden (fig. 80).[5] It suggested to him the idea of a protesting crowd in front of the flat horizontal line of the podium, the more detailed architectural perspective to the left, and, indeed, the shapes of certain doors and win-

89

Fig. 81. Marcantonio after Bandinelli. The Martyrdom of St. Lawrence.
[Engraving]

dows. But Lucas van Leyden's engraving is a purely graphic invention, detailed and diffuse, whereas Rembrandt's etching has the unified structure of a composition which could be enlarged till it filled a whole wall. There is something Florentine in the uncompromising geometry of the architecture; and in fact one of the sources of Rembrandt's composition seems to have been Florentine, a once famous engraving by Marcantonio of the martyrdom of St. Lawrence (fig. 81) after a design by Bandinelli. It, too, makes the impression of a stage set, with crowds of animated figures at various levels, the judge raised on a frontal podium, the surrounding architecture severe and claustrophobic. The two arches on either side do not at first appear in Rembrandt's design; but they evidently made a deep impression on him, for in order to get them off his mind he made, in later states of the etching, one of the most extravagant of all his alterations (fig. 82). Once more a powerful intellectual construction is sacrificed to an imperative dream. The crowd, that marvellous cross-section of humanity, shoving and gesticulating round the base of the podium, is removed, save for two figures peering anxiously round the corners; and in its place appear the two arches, shaggy, rusticated, ir-

90

Fig. 82. Rembrandt. Christ Presented to the People (1655). [Etching, 7th state]

regular, the greatest possible contrast to the trim abstraction of the earlier design. They are like the doors of a Piranesian dungeon, or conduits leading to some *cloaca maxima*, orifices through which we enter those portions of human economy which lie hidden from our consciousness. Between these arches is a shadowy figure, whose flowing beard and braided hair are those of an antique river god, and who rests his arm on a pitcher; but his pensive pose is unmistakably Michelangelesque (fig. 83). The Moses inspired the movement of his left arm; his right hand, supporting his bearded chin, echoes the Jeremiah of the Sistine. We know that Rembrandt owned a book "full of the work of Michelangelo Buonarotti" (inv. no. 230) but references to Michelangelo in his work are extremely rare. It was possible to absorb the science of Raphael without copying his imagery; but Michelangelo's heroic idealisation of humanity was less easy to digest. The sudden emergence of this deep mysterious note, and its almost immediate subsidence (for in only a few impressions of the sixth state is the river god clearly discernable) cannot, I think, be explained by iconographical arguments, but may well be connected with the Michelangelesque tensions of the architecture; indeed I am inclined to think that the book full of Michelangelo's work contained the print by Antonio da Salamanca (1554) which shows the Julius monument in S. Pietro in

Fig. 83. Rembrandt. Detail of Christ Presented to the People (1655). [Etching, 6th state]

92

Fig. 84. Antonio da Salamanca. Michelangelo's monument to Julius II. [Engraving]

Vincoli (fig. 84). Rembrandt was at first interested in the architecture, especially the terms with wedge-shaped bases; but the pull of the Moses was too strong for him, and one reason why he emptied the lower part of his structure was in order that this compulsive figure should appear.

The year after the etching of Christ Presented to the People, Rembrandt was once more able to work on a monumental scale. The subject was that with which he had first made his name, an anatomy lesson. It was painted for the anatomical theatre of Amsterdam, and the lecturer was named Dr. Joan Deyman. This was originally a very large picture, but in 1823 it was damaged by fire, and only a fragment remains, which is now in the Rijksmuseum (fig. 85). Fortunately there also exists a small

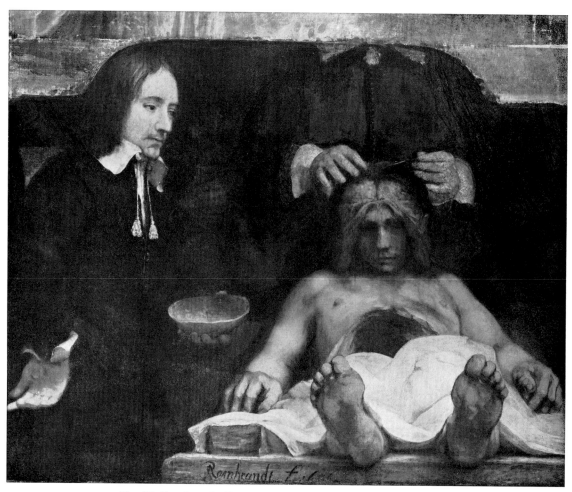

Fig. 85. Rembrandt. Dr. Deyman's Anatomy Lesson. (Fragment)

drawing of the whole composition, summary and almost diagramatic, but vividly authentic (fig. 86);[6] and from this chance survival we can form some idea of Rembrandt's most calculated design. At the centre was a tribute to renaissance art-theory, for a nude figure, frontal and in steep foreshortening, was, so to say, the hero of Quattrocento perspective, and remained, for almost a century after the time of Uccello, a kind of diploma of perfection in renaissance art. As with the profile (see p. 72), Rembrandt did not use this violent foreshortening simply as a technical exercise, but as a way of heightening our emotions. In this it is tempting to suppose that he had been influenced by one of the most moving pieces of

94

Fig. 86. Rembrandt. Suggestions for the frame of Dr. Deyman's Anatomy Lesson. [Drawing]

foreshortening in art, Mantegna's Dead Christ now in the Brera (fig. 87). He could have known one of several versions of the original,[7] or perhaps a study for it, similar to the drawing of a foreshortened man in the British Museum. At all events he has given his central figure the pathos and solemnity of a *pietà*. Involuntarily we look for the stigmata on hands and feet. We must remember that in the seventeenth century the dissection of a corpse was still a rare and somewhat awful event, and that many early anatomy theatres were set up in abandoned chapels.[8] Whether or not Rembrandt was conscious of this feeling it is hard to say: there is little sign of it in the earlier Anatomy of Dr. Tulp. But as far as we can judge from the drawing, the whole picture was conceived in these solemn terms. Dr. Deyman rose behind the corpse like the celebrant of some religious rite, and his assistant, fortunately preserved, has the solicitude of an aco-

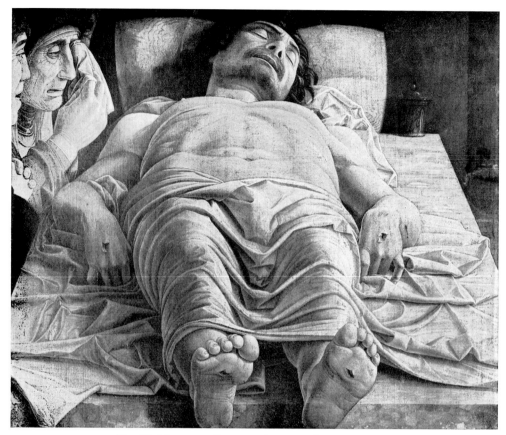

Fig. 87. Mantegna. Lamentation over the Dead Christ

lyte. Behind him the spectators sit and stand as if in the apse of a church and even the indecipherable emblem over Dr. Deyman's head is reminiscent of a crucifix.

The design of Dr. Deyman's Anatomy Lesson, symmetrical and hieratic, its frontality modified by the curve of the apse, shows Rembrandt deeply involved in the mediterranean tradition. Unconsciously it goes back to the early Christian mosaic at Santa Pudenziana. When six years later he was commissioned to paint another large group portrait, the picture known as The Syndics (fig 53.), he returned to a more traditional form. It is true, as I have said (p. 62), that the grouping owes something to Leonardo's Last Supper, and that the low point of vision shows a mastery of perspective which could hardly have been achieved without a study of Italian science. In general disposition, however, The Syndics does not depart far from old models such as Nicholas Elias' Regents of the Spinhuis.[9] Many critics have commented on its rare tranquility, and this may in part be due to the fact that Rembrandt has calmly accepted the limitations of an earlier Dutch tradition. But in 1656, having demonstrated his mastery of the Italian science of picture-making on a monumental scale, Rembrandt must have felt himself fully capable of undertaking a great scheme of decoration in the renaissance manner. In these years the opportunity for such a scheme presented itself. By 1655 the new Town Hall of Amsterdam, begun by van Campen in 1648, had reached the point when plans had been prepared for its decoration.[10] Since he had been passed over in the scheme for decorating the Huis ten Bosch, Rembrandt cannot have expected to be given a large share in this even more heavily official enterprise. Not only were the connoisseurs against him, but high academic opinion, led by the poet Joost van Vondel, was set on something in the ideal baroque manner, with plenty of allegories and personifications. However, as an appendix to all this abstraction there was to be a series of eight gigantic paintings representing episodes in the supposed origins of the Dutch nation, the revolt of the Batavians against Rome, that was of course seen as the prototype of their recent successful revolt against Spain. This series was entrusted to Govaert Flinck, and only because he died before his sketches could be executed did the city fathers turn to Rembrandt. He was then (1661) allotted the first of the series, a scene described by Tacitus (*Histories*, IV, 14) in which the leader of the Batavians, Claudius Civilis, invites his countrymen to a midnight banquet and persuades them to swear an oath of rebellion against the Romans.

This scene of poetic drama, drawn from a legendary past, untramelled by antiquarian circumstance, free from allegory or precedent,[11] must have stirred Rembrandt's imagination profoundly; and we may suppose that the result was in many ways his greatest painting. But once more, only a fragment survives (fig. 88). In 1662, soon after it was put in place, the original canvas was given back to Rembrandt for no recorded reason. It never returned to the Town Hall, and its place was taken by a mediocre work by Ovens, painted over Flinck's cartoon. In the end Rembrandt cut out the central group, reworked it in his latest style and produced the picture that is now in Stockholm. Splendid though this is, it can convey

Fig. 88. Rembrandt. The Conspiracy of Claudius Civilis. (Fragment)

only a small part of the dramatic poetry of the original, and with the help of a drawing in Munich (fig. 89) we must try to imagine what the whole composition was like. Rembrandt has pictured the meeting taking place in a vaulted ruin, open to the sky, like the Baths of Caracalla. Across one arch, as a background to the feast, hung a brocaded curtain; above it and to the side, trees stood out against a moonlit sky. The group of conspirators, lit by an unseen flare, were encircled by the dark and majestic vegetation of the primeval world. We can guess from the background of the equestrian portrait in the National Gallery that these nocturnal details would have been handled with an evocative breadth equalled only by Titian in his old age. The Claudius Civilis must have been the supreme example in Rembrandt's work of that Venetian mood which I discuss in the next chapter, and there may even have been some distant memory of Paul Veronese's great banquets, in the way that the foreground figures come up stairs from below, and are silhouetted against the table. But what a contrast to the lordly company in the house of Levi! Nowhere, to judge from

98

the fragment at Stockholm, has Rembrandt gone further from the ideals of mediterranean art, both in imagery and technique. The sense of ideal form, which underlies Paul Veronese's portrayal of the human figure, even at his most pictorial, has entirely vanished, and the forms seem to be dissolved in light; or, rather, light becomes the means of revealing their expressive possibilities. Dramatically it is an extreme example of that anti-classical imagery which, as I said earlier, persisted throughout Rembrandt's work, and was almost unaffected by his mastery of classical design. Nowhere else does he come so recklessly near to the absurd and achieve the sublime. The facile comparison of Rembrandt with Shakespeare, frequently attempted, is seldom apt; in their attitudes to religion and morality alone they were as different as it is possible for two supremely great men to be. But in this instance the word Shakespearean is irresistable. Rembrandt has evoked the kind of quasi-mythical, heroico-magical past which is the setting for *Macbeth*, *King Lear* and *Cvmbeline;* and, as with Shakespeare, this remoteness has allowed him to insert into an episode of primitive grandeur the life-giving roughage of the grotesque. The characters at the extreme ends of the table, to left and right, are equivalent

Fig. 89. Rembrandt. Study for Conspiracy of
Claudius Civilis. [Drawing]

to the grave-diggers in *Hamlet* or the porter in *Macbeth;* and just as the unclassical elements in the plays are sustained by a dazzling beauty of language, so Rembrandt's Batavians are transfigured by paint of the most exquisite colour and texture.

Rouault and the expressionists have enabled us to take these figures seriously, but it would be surprising if the city fathers of Amsterdam had not found them disconcerting;[12] and the decision to reject Rembrandt's masterpiece does not require any elaborate explanation. In reaction from the established view that the last fifteen years of Rembrandt's life were passed in total oblivion, recent scholars have been intent on proving that he was still appreciated, and that even the return of his Claudius Civilis was due to changes of architecture in the Town Hall, rather than to changes of taste.[13] It is true that he maintained a high reputation as a face-painter and received a number of portrait commissions, including The Syndics. His drawings and etchings were also collected and praised for their liveliness. But as a painter of biblical and historical scenes he was not taken seriously. Sandrart, who says that Rembrandt could paint old people with wrinkles and cabinet pictures with elegant costumes, was certainly voicing contemporary opinion, and for two hundred years posterity agreed with him. This misunderstanding of Rembrandt's genius involved an incalculable loss to the world. If the great conceptions of his later drawings and etchings had been carried out on the scale implicit in their design we should have had a series of masterpieces unlike anything else in art, rich, mysterious, human, evocative, and yet constructed with the architectural logic of a renaissance fresco.

4

Rembrandt and the Venetians

I have said that Rembrandt's determination to master the laws of classic art was complementary to that other side of his character which, in default of a better word, I have called romantic. The finest of his early works, like the Rape of Proserpine (fig. 7) or the Samson and Delilah (fig. 20), are romantic poems expressed through light and colour; and we might have supposed that in this field Rembrandt had no need of masters. But here, too, he developed his prodigious talents by the study of the Italian Renaissance, with Giorgione and Titian taking the place of Raphael and Leonardo. Venetian art had on Rembrandt an influence of a very different kind from that of Roman or Florentine. When borrowing a classic motive from a Marcantonio engraving he practically always changed the subject, and often modified the form in a way which revealed a long and enlightening process of thought. But he felt so much in sympathy with the imaginative world of Titian and Giorgione that when he took over one of their motives he usually retained the subject and even vestiges of the style. In consequence his borrowings from Venetian art are more obvious and less interesting than his borrowings from Raphael, and have long been familiar to all writers on Rembrandt (fig. 90).[1]

Unlike Roman and Florentine art, which he knew almost entirely from prints and drawings, Rembrandt knew Venetian art at first hand, from original pictures. It was impossible to send Raphael's frescoes to Amsterdam for sale, but it was possible to send the masterpieces of Titian; and they came in almost unbelievable quantities. A few we can identify; many are lost. The percentage of famous works of art which somehow managed to disappear between 1640 and 1840, when scientific cataloguing began,

Fig. 90. Rembrandt. Virgin with the Instruments of the Passion. [Etching]

is a constant source of surprise; and in assessing Rembrandt's debt to Venetian art we must remember how incomplete and fragmentary is our knowledge of his sources. The gallery of Andrea Vendramin provides an impressive warning. This famous collection was brought to Amsterdam in the 1640's, and the sale was handled by Saskia's cousin, Gerritt van Uylenburgh. Rembrandt must have known it well. It contained works by Bellini, Giorgione, Titian, Paris Bordone, both the Palmas, Schiavone, Tintoretto and several minor Venetians. Fortunately Vendramin had made

102

Fig. 91. Rembrandt. Christ Driving out the Money Changers

a manuscript catalogue of his collection, with illustrations of each item,[2] which give us a fair notion of what they were like; and of the hundred and fifty-five pictures illustrated, only four can be identified today; the rest have simply vanished. If this was the wastage in a single collection, we are justified in assuming that many Venetian pictures were known to Rembrandt which are unknown to us, and we should not be debarred from claiming a Venetian origin for some of his ideas because no original exists.

In addition to the numerous Venetian pictures passing through the Amsterdam art market, many of which were no doubt copied in the atelier of Hendrick van Uylenburgh (see note 212) and were thus available for study even after they had been sold, Rembrandt owned what is described in the inventory as a "very large book," with nearly all the works of Titian.[3] These were, presumably, engravings after Titian's paintings, especially the series engraved by Cornelius Cort, published in the sixteenth century. But Cort's engravings alone would not fill a "very large" book, and probably it contained a number of woodcuts by Boldrini and others; also, as we shall see, drawings by Titian and his school.

There are Venetian echoes in works of the 1630's and not surprisingly the painters whose influence is most often identifiable are members of the Bassano family. The very earliest of Rembrandt's quotations from Italian

Fig. 92. Rembrandt. Christ Driving out the Money Changers.
[Etching]

104

Fig. 93. Rembrandt. The Angel Appearing to the Shepherds. [Etching]

art is to be found in a small panel in the Pushkin Museum, the expulsion
of the Money Changers, signed and dated 1626 (fig. 91), which, although
doubted by the museum authorities, is clearly authentic.[4] The leading
money changer leaves us in no doubt that Rembrandt knew one of

105

Fig. 94. Rembrandt. Belshazzar's Feast

Jacopo Bassano's numerous versions of the subject.[5] He is the figure traditionally identified as a likeness of Titian, who also appears in the version of the subject in the National Gallery, London; but in the Rembrandt he is wearing Titian's characteristic black fur-lined cloak. As the figure is in reverse he is probably taken from an engraving. When, nine years later, Rembrandt returned to the subject in an etching (fig. 92), the example of Bassano was still in his mind. The figure of Christ is taken from Dürer's Small Passion (B. 23), but the diagonal composition and the stampeding animals are still openly Bassanesque, and Rembrandt has even (most exceptionally) left one of the figures in Venetian costume. No doubt it was this bustle and animation which first attracted him in Bassano, but he was also impressed by the Bassani's mastery of night pieces, with effects of candle-light and fire. The inventory of Rembrandt's collection records (no. 54) *een brandent leger van den oude Bassan*, where *leger* presumably means a pen or enclosure of animals; and an echo of this scene, with the terrified cattle struggling to escape from the flames, is to be found in what was once the most famous of Rembrandt's early etchings (fig. 93), the Angel appearing to the Shepherds (1634), where the heavenly apparition has produced a similar panic: a good example of Rembrandt using the evidence of a natural occurrence to illustrate a supernatural event.[6]

The two tricks which Rembrandt could learn from the Bassani, crowds in movement and artificial light, were soon mastered, and decisively surpassed; and already in the 1630's he had begun to absorb the far more potent influence of Titian. It is apparent in two large paintings of the period, both clearly done for his own satisfaction (one of them, perhaps, never sold[7]), the Belshazzar's Feast in the National Gallery (fig. 94) and the Danae in the Hermitage. The date in the Belshazzar has been erased, but the picture must be considerably earlier than Dr. Tulp's Anatomy Lesson (1632) and, although superbly effective, has faults which Rem-

Fig. 95. Paul Veronese. The Rape of Europa.
(Detail)

Fig. 96. Titian. Bacchanal of the Andrians.
(Detail)

brandt soon learned to avoid. The diagonal of Belshazzar's right arm cuts too sharply across the design; the centre, with its pool of darkness under Belshazzar's cloak, is empty; above all, there is an inconsistency of style between the group on the left, brilliantly observed, and the Italianate figure of a reveller on the right, who, in this setting, is too obviously a creation of art. She is clearly inspired by Venetian painting, and may have been taken direct from the woman helping Europa to keep her seat on the bull in Paul Veronese's picture in the Ducal Palace (fig. 95), known through a drawing or copy. No doubt Rembrandt was impressed by this piece of foreshortening, executed with such easy skill; but the wine jar in the reveller's hand shows that he was also aware of an earlier Venetian foreshortening, the woman of Andros on the ground in Titian's Bacchanal (fig. 96), presumably known from an engraving, for the figure is reversed; and it was this secondary association with drunken revelry which made him use a similar pose in the Belshazzar.

For once the woman is not completely absorbed into the world of Rembrandt's imagination, and is even painted with an academic anxiety unusual in his work after 1630. The Danae (fig. 97), on the other hand, is one of the most beautiful and harmonious of all Rembrandt's early pictures. Once more his point of departure was a synthesis of two Titian figures, a Venus similar to that in the Uffizi (fig. 98) and a Danae like those in Naples and the Prado. Both pictures were much copied in the sixteenth century, and Rembrandt could easily have known studio replicas. The left arm, with its bracelets, resting on a pillow, appears in both of them, and Rembrandt has repeated it, with minor changes. But how far he has departed from his originals both in sentiment and form! The head of Titian's Venus is without expression; and her body is inert and self-contained, a kind of monstrous fruit, incapable of movement or sensation. The Danae is warm, responsive, open, outward turning. Her gaze and the gesture of her hand, at once welcoming, defensive and surprised, have the complexity of a real human response, and her body is equally far from the vegetable inertia of Titian's Venus. It is more sensuously compelling, partly because it is more natural, and partly because the light, which she greets as her lover, passes over her body like a caressing hand.

Books on Rembrandt usually describe the Danae as a likeness of Saskia, although it seems improbable that the daughter of the Burgomaster of

108

Fig. 97. Rembrandt. Danae

Fig. 98. Titian. Venus and Cupid

Leeuwarden would have allowed herself to be portrayed in these circumstances, and comparison with the numerous, undoubted portraits of Saskia is by no means convincing. I suppose we can reasonably assume that the tender sensuality of the Danae was a result of Rembrandt's first happy years of marriage; but a naive concordance between the known facts of his life, almost as unrevealing as those of Shakespeare, and the abundant, but debatable, evidence of his works is often misleading. For eight years after painting the Danae Rembrandt did not return to this vein of intimate tenderness,[8] and paradoxically enough it was only after the death of Saskia in 1644 that this particular sentiment once more colours his work. There follow those two poems of domestic happiness, the Holy Families at Leningrad and Cassel (fig. 62). A new emotional tranquillity seems to have opened his mind to all that is fruitful and harmonious in nature and he began to enjoy the charm of the Amsterdam countryside. Most of the landscape drawings are direct notations made on the spot, from which we can follow his daily walks. But in the etchings, where he gathers these im-

110

pressions together, Rembrandt makes use of those devices of lighting and grouping by which the sixteenth-century Venetians had first brought the irregularities of nature into a single focus. The etching of a landscape with a tower and barn (fig. 99), by the gentle undulation of the ground, the line of the roofs, the very way the light falls on the wall and thatch of the barn, achieves that kind of poetry which we call Giorgionesque; and like other similarities in Rembrandt's work this is not the result of accident, but of study.

Fig. 99. Rembrandt. Landscape with a Tower. [Etching]

Rembrandt undoubtedly owned a number of those prints and drawings of landscape which were done in sixteenth-century Venice under the influence of Titian. There were woodcuts, like those of Ugo da Carpi and Boldrini, with their rocky escarpments and thick, fleshy tree trunks; and there were drawings of the kind now ascribed to Domenico Campagnola, which skilfully led the eye back from the figures in the foreground, over an artfully modelled middle distance, to a background of farm buildings or a castle on a hill. How resolutely he made this style his own is shown by a curious example, a Venetian landscape drawing in Budapest (fig. 101)[9] which certainly belonged to Rembrandt as he has gone over it with the same bold strokes that he used to correct his pupils' drawings. Only a short step in the direction of naturalism separates it from a characteristic Rembrandt landscape, such as that in fig. 100; and in comparing these two we begin to understand why Rembrandt, with his unequalled gifts of direct notation, yet felt the need to master a way of rendering landscape

111

Fig. 100. Rembrandt. Landscape. [Drawing]

Fig. 101. Rembrandt over Campagnola. Landscape. [Drawing]

112

by which the terrain was modelled more firmly and the eye was concentrated on a single unit of trees and buildings. This lesson he then applied to his own observations, giving them a more poetic and, so to say, ideal character, but very seldom betraying by an obvious reference how much the Venetian *poesie* had influenced his style (fig. 102)[10]. There was, moreover, a certain mood which the Venetians had made so much their own that no painter with Rembrandt's sympathetic imagination could have failed to be influenced by their vision: I mean the mood of sentimental involvement with the time of day, the quality of light, the colour of the sky, all those aspects of nature which seem to reflect our thoughts and symbolise our

Fig. 102. Rembrandt. Rest in the Flight. [Drawing]

emotions. This achievement of art, which Ruskin called the pathetic fallacy, was almost the discovery of Giorgione,[11] and from his time onwards was associated with certain episodes in the Bible where a phrase, or sometimes only a couple of words, suggests that nature is participating in a divine revelation. Christ and the Samaritan woman by the well, the walk to Emmaus, *Noli me Tangere:* these are subjects in which landscape is no longer merely a background, but a protagonist; and Rembrandt, in treating these themes, did not disguise his indebtedness to the Venetian

Fig. 103. Giulio Campagnola. Christ and the Woman of Samaria. [Engraving]

discovery. He owned a large picture of Christ and the Woman of Samaria
which he attributed to Giorgione (inv. no. 109), and he probably knew at
least one other Giorgionesque version of the subject, an engraving by
Giulio Campagnola (fig. 103). This design is usually attributed to Sebastiano del Piombo,[12] but it is completely Giorgionesque in spirit, and the
figures are so similar to those in the Glasgow Christ and the Adulteress—
which seems, on balance, to be a Giorgione finished by Titian—that it
may even be derived from a companion picture. There are at least ten
representations of Christ and the Adulteress in Rembrandt's work, four
paintings, four drawings and two etchings, and they show a great diversity
of treatment. But all, except the early etching, are entirely Venetian in
spirit, and some of them, like the etching of 1658 (fig. 104), with its rich
Paris Bordone landscape, suggest some unidentified Venetian original.

One thing they all have in common is the prominence of the well. From
the beautiful drawing in the Barber Institute, Birmingham (fig. 105), to
the late etching, it dominates the foreground and seems to be the real sub-

114

Fig. 104. Rembrandt. Christ and the Woman of Samaria. [Etching]

ject of conversation between the Samaritan woman and Our Lord. Rembrandt, who was much better versed in Christian symbolism than used to be supposed, knew that the well was a symbol of purification and virginity; and we feel that he had also recognised its compositional value, and used it as a *repoussoir*, a firm, cylindrical block round which the surrounding greenery could freely expand. He may also have shared the Venetian feeling for the cool invisible depths of the well and melodious trickle of water, which Pater perceptively recognised as the *continuo* of Giorgionesque poetry.

In addition to these lyrical episodes in the Bible, which gave the Venetians the opportunity for mood-landscapes, there was one traditional

Fig. 105. Rembrandt. Christ and the Woman of Samaria. [Drawing]

subject which allowed them to represent nature unconstrained, the saint in the wilderness. The Venetian conception of this scene followed a curious precedent which dates back to Giovanni Bellini. Instead of a real desert, Bellini had placed his saints in the earthly paradise of the Veneto, and Titian had surrounded them by nature in her most fruitful and generative mood. Whether consciously or unconsciously, it was this contrast between the

116

Fig. 106. Rembrandt. St. Jerome in a Landscape. [Etching]

health and organic harmony of great trees and the spiritual struggle of renunciation which led him to return so often to the subject. Saints in the wilderness are the subject of two of Rembrandt's finest etchings, the St. Jerome of 1653 (fig. 106) and the St. Francis of 1657 (fig. 110). Once more he goes back, in imagery if not in design, to Giorgione; for Michiel, the earliest and most reliable authority on Venetian painting, records the existence of two paintings by Giorgione of St. Jerome seated in a landscape, one of them in moonlight.[13] Of these no trace remains; but at least four of Titian's renderings of the subject can be identified, two pictures in the

117

Fig. 107. Cornelius Cort.
St. Jerome in a Landscape. [Engraving]

Fig. 108. Campagnola? Figures in Landscape.
[Drawing]

Louvre and Milan, which were probably unknown to Rembrandt,[14] and two engravings, which he undoubtedly knew. One of these is by Cornelius Cort (fig. 107) and, like Rembrandt's etching, it shows St. Jerome seated contemplating the scriptures. Titian had imagined him as a hero-saint in Michelangelesque pose, and this Rembrandt has rejected, thinking instead of a quiet scholar, as Giovanni Bellini might have pictured him, in cardinal's hat and cassock; but he has retained the watchful lion and the escarpment of high rocks, with a tree growing out of it. He must also have known a drawing connected with Cort's engraving (although with pagan figures), of which there is a replica in the Ecole des Beaux-Arts, Paris (fig. 108), and has taken from it the composition and the rustic building on the hill.

The other Titian of St. Jerome which is known to us from an engraving (fig. 109) shows the saint kneeling in front of a tree to which he has tied his crucifix. Rembrandt has used the same motive in his etching of 1657,

Fig. 109. After Titian. St. Jerome in a Landscape. [Engraving]

119

Fig. 110. Rembrandt. St. Francis in a Landscape. [Etching]

but has changed the St. Jerome into a St. Francis (fig. 110), and has made the whole scene far more dramatic. The tree which thrusts itself between the saint and his crucifix is apparently drawn from nature; and the saint himself is a counter-reformation figure, closer to Baroccio than to Titian; but the contrast of natural and spiritual energy goes back to the great Venetians.

In the preparatory drawing for his etching of St. Jerome (fig. 111) Rembrandt comes nearer to the Venetian style than anywhere else in his work. Not only is there a similarity of mood and design, but the actual technique is suggestive of Titian, although we must admit that no similar drawing by Titian has come down to us. It is true that great colourists, using line to suggest colour, nearly all arrive at a similar pen technique, with broken line and free, light-promoting contours. Giovanni Bellini's drawings are sometimes surprisingly Rembrandtesque. But the technical similarities between Rembrandt's and Titian's drawings go further than this. A famous

120

Fig. 111. Rembrandt. St. Jerome Reading in a Landscape. [Drawing]

Fig. 112. Titian. An Old Man Seated. [Drawing]

Titian drawing in the Uffizi of an old man seated (fig. 112) is so like a Rembrandt in the actual handwriting, that it has even been claimed as Rembrandt's work. And it is precisely in certain Venetian subjects that we are most conscious of Rembrandt using Titianesque technique. An interesting example is a late drawing in Dresden of Diana and Acteon (fig. 113). It has been frequently observed that this composition is related to an etching by Pietro Testa, but neither the style nor the design bear any relationship to Testa's playful etching; they are, on the other hand, extremely close to Titian, or one of his pupils such as Schiavone, and it

122

Fig. 113. Rembrandt. Diana and Acteon. [Drawing]

seems possible that both the Testa and the Rembrandt drawing go back
to a lost design by Titian.

Rembrandt's debt to the Venetians was not limited to landscape. As a
portrait painter he learnt professional wisdom from the first masters of the
life-size portrait; and in his later work he was inspired by Giorgionesque
discoveries to paint figures which have no ostensible subject, but touch the
imagination by a mysterious play of colour and light. Like all successful
portrait painters, he was always on the look-out for fresh poses. In the
1630's he tried most of the current formulae: the hand on the breast of
Van Dyck (although with a very different effect), the communicative
gesture of Frans Hals, the diagonal pose of Rubens, as well as some admirable inventions of his own; but on the whole there is very little in his
early portraiture that recalls Titian. But towards the end of the decade

123

Fig. 114. Titian. Porait of a Man   Fig. 115. Raphael. Portrait of Castiglione

there appeared in the Amsterdam art market Titian's so-called portrait of Ariosto (fig. 114). This is one of the most perfect early solutions of life-size portraiture, and we can imagine how its balance and completeness appealed to Rembrandt at a time when he was already beginning to look for a greater equilibrium. It so happened that in the same year another masterpiece of early sixteenth-century portrait painting was offered for sale in Amsterdam, Raphael's Baldassare Castiglione (fig. 115). To include the Castiglione in this chapter is not so paradoxical as it seems, because in it Raphael has consciously adopted the Venetian style. Giorgione was one of Castiglione's favourite artists, and the talents of his successor, the still youthful Titian, had been praised in Roman society by that arbiter of taste, Pietro Bembo. Several of his works had reached Rome, and had so much impressed the all-absorbing Raphael that he had re-painted the Swiss Guards in the Mass of Bolsena in a colouristic manner. In the portrait of his friend, Castiglione, he used the canvas support, the pose and the subtle colour of the Venetians in a calculated and entirely successful attempt to equal his northern rival.[15] So these two great masterpieces of

124

the early Venetian portrait style were both in Amsterdam in 1639; in fact, they were in the same collection, that of a Spaniard named Alfonso Lopez; and Rembrandt made good use of them. On April 9th he went to the auction where the Castiglione was sold, and made a sketch of it (fig. 116), on which he noted that it fetched 3,500 guilders. He then attempted to combine the pose of the Raphael with that of the Titian, retaining from the Venetian picture the parapet, the position of the arm and the splendid shining sleeve; but taking from the Raphael the turn of the head and the black beret. The result was the etching of himself (fig. 117) done in the same year, 1639, which is the classic image of Rembrandt in prosperity. It is remarkable that he has made the Titian the basis of a self-portrait, because the pose of the so-called Ariosto has suggested to a recent scholar[16] that this is itself a self-portrait of Titian, and this feeling may have communicated itself to Rembrandt. It is also revealing to see how strongly the rakish angle of the cap was established in Rembrandt's inner eye, so that

Fig. 116. Rembrandt. Copy of Raphael's Castiglione (detail) [Pen and wash]

Fig. 117. Rembrandt. Self-portrait Leaning on a Sill (1639) [Etching, 1st state]

125

Fig. 118. Rembrandt. Self-portrait Leaning on a Sill (1640)

Fig. 119. Portrait of Saskia (? posthumous)

he even imposes it on his copy of the Castiglione, thereby changing its static presence into something far less severe. The etching did not exhaust his interest in Raphael's masterpiece, and in the following year he painted the famous self-portrait in the National Gallery, London (fig. 118), in which Titian's quilted sleeve is replaced by the curving outline of a cloak, and our interest is concentrated on the head. The sleeve he used again in a portrait of a man in the Duke of Westminster's collection.

From this time forward Rembrandt's portraits show an increasing interest in Venetian types and poses. He continued to use the window-sill formula of early Venetian portraiture, as in a beautiful drawing at Bayonne, the most Giorgionesque of all his figure pieces. In what is perhaps a posthumous portrait of Saskia (fig. 119) he uses the cut-off bust, with straight neckline and chain, which may have been an invention of Bellini, although the hand on the breast seems to have been introduced by Giorgione in his portrait of Brocardo. In the 1650's he studied the mature Titian, so that his noble portrait, in Washington, of a young woman

127

Fig. 120. Rembrandt. Portrait of a Lady with a Pink

Fig. 121. Rembrandt. Self-portrait (1658)

with a pink (fig. 120) is really a feminine counterpart of *L'homme au gant*. Nor was Titian the only influence; the portrait of an old man recently acquired for the London National Gallery is in a pose derived from Tintoretto. And in several of Rembrandt's greatest portraits we feel the Venetian spirit permeating the whole design although we cannot point to the individual Titian or Tintoretto on which they are based. In the superb self-portrait painted in the year of his bankruptcy (fig. 121)—a philosopher king indifferent to misfortune—not only is the grandiose, frontal pose derived from Titian, but the pleated shirt is a part of Venetian sixteenth-century dress, which Rembrandt has put on, partly because he felt like dressing up, and partly because it gave him a strong horizontal line.

But in spite of similarities of design, the basis of Rembrandt's portraiture was very different from that of Titian. It may seem far-fetched to speak of Catholic and Protestant portraiture, but it is a fact that Titian's strongly Catholic approach to all experience, his hearty acceptance of doctrine and hierarchy, is perceptible in his attitude toward his sitters, and even in his sense of form. He saw each sitter as a type to be enhanced till it reached its perfect state, rather as our bodies will be (the theologians tell us) on the Day of Judgement. Rembrandt, who was essentially a Protestant, saw each sitter as an individual human soul whose weaknesses and imperfections must not be disguised, because they are the raw material of grace. It was this pre-occupation with the individual which led him to study his own face so relentlessly. He was himself the only sitter who could reveal all the ups and downs of confidence, the shining and obfuscation of inner light, which go to make up the individual soul; and the knowledge thus acquired enabled him to grasp and concentrate on the spiritual state of each sitter. How infinitely subtle and bafflingly complex is the character who gazes at us from the late self-portrait in the Rijksmuseum (fig. 122) and how arrogantly external by comparison are the self-portraits of Titian. And yet, the pictorial inventiveness of Venetian art was irresistible to him, so that he derived ideas for portraits from the most unlikely sources. Two examples will show how he could relate Venetian motives to direct experience in the same way he had translated the "judicious inventions" of Raphael.

The Vendramin Collection contained several of those pictures representing ample, uncorseted ladies, who are, perhaps, not sufficiently ath-

Fig. 122. Rembrandt. Self-portrait (1661)

Fig. 123. Illustration to the Vendramin Catalogue

letic for modern taste, but who obviously appealed to Venetian amateurs in the mid-sixteenth century. One of them, on folio 51 of the manuscript catalogue (fig. 123), is of a type generally described as by Palma Vecchio, of which, in fact, two versions still survive.[17] Rembrandt has not been interested by the implications of the subject, but he has been delighted with the circular movement of the pose, and has seen how it could give a new character to the window-frame device, which he had already used several times. Thus, from a cloying and artificial formula he has made one of the most fresh and natural of all his portraits, the picture of Hendrickje in Berlin (fig. 124). It happens that twenty years earlier, the first and most famous of all these Venetian beauties was to be seen in Amsterdam, also in the collection of Alfonso Lopez, Titian's Flora (fig. 125). Rembrandt was delighted by this version of pagan opulence and determined to equal

132

Fig. 124. Rembrandt. Hendrickje at the Window

Fig. 125. Titian. Flora

it. But in 1633, when he painted Saskia as Flora (fig. 126), he had not yet understood that the sensuous appeal of the Titian lay to some extent in the extreme simplicity of the means, the large areas of white linen, the almost equal area of radiant flesh, with the hands alone providing two points of denser modelling. Rembrandt in his exuberance decided to dress up his bride in much richer materials, to give her a much larger bunch of flowers. He wanted, in every sense of the words, to lay it on thick; and faced with this amiable apparition, we are grateful for his extravagance. Eight years later he is in a more soberly domestic frame of mind, but he has not forgotten the pose of the Flora, and so he treats it exactly as he was to treat the Palma in the Vendramin Collection: he uses it as the basis of a portrait in contemporary costume, the picture of Saskia in Dresden

134

Fig. 126. Rembrandt. Saskia as Flora

Fig. 127. Rembrandt. Portrait of Saskia

Fig. 128. Rembrandt. Hendrickje as Flora

(fig. 127). Finally, about 1656, he returns to the subject of Flora in the enchanting portrait of Hendrickje in the Metropolitan Museum, New York (fig. 128). By now he has learnt the value of simple planes and the areas of light and dark are similar to those of Titian. Rembrandt has understood the pictorial meaning of the Flora, not merely been excited by its imagery. He has also invented his own world of forms which after 1650 became basically rectangular, built up of shallow cubes (see p. 180); whereas Titian's form-world is basically ovoid, and always develops a curved surface.

Beyond the greater consistency of design is a consistency of vision. The slightly ludicrous, almost touching, discrepancy between the clothes and the persons they encase, evident in the National Gallery Flora, and even

137

Fig. 129. Rembrandt. Bellona

more pronounced in a picture of Bellona, in the Metropolitan (fig. 129), was, after all, due to a failure of unifying imagination. The trappings belong to a world of fantasy, are indeed a belated display of mannerist accomplishment. The persons belong to the world of experience—not simply visual experience, but daily human contact—and are represented without any mitigation which might bring their homely features into harmony with their splendid accoutrements. Fifteen years later than the Metropolitan Bellona, he painted the armed figure (its intention is uncertain) in the Gulbenkian Collection (fig. 130). The beautiful head is half

138

Fig. 130. Rembrandt. "Minerva"

in shadow, and so unemphatic that scholars are unable to decide whether it is a man or a woman, Mars, Minerva or Alexander the Great. By its mood it frees our minds for the contemplation of the helmet. This helmet is a marvellous child of Rembrandt's imagination, completely re-created in paint; and the rich facture is used to express emotions very different from the cheerful confidence in craftsmanship which is the chief condition of the earlier armour pieces. It is a deeply personal picture; and yet the whole idea of a handsome shadowy face, mysteriously subordinated to shining armour, was unquestionably one of the innovations of Giorgione; and in this instance Rembrandt seems to have had an actual picture in mind, feeble enough if we can judge from the copy in the Vendramin Catalogue (fig. 131): a figure in armour, also of indeterminate sex, there attributed to Paris Bordone.

Fig. 131. Illustration to the Vendramin Catalogue

At the beginning of this book I mentioned Livingstone Lowes' rich, discursive study of the creative process. It uncovered the layers of association which go to the making of a masterpiece; it suggested that great works of art can be (and indeed usually are) involved with memories of other works of art; and it showed how the accident—which is never quite

140

Fig. 132. Rembrandt. The Jewish Bride

an accident—of a subject or a commission can suddenly release these memories and concentrate them, so that they transform direct experience. I mention this study of Coleridge again because the picture which I shall now examine, the picture known as The Jewish Bride (fig. 132), has the magic of a great poetic utterance. Of all Rembrandt's works it is the most haunting and draws upon emotions from the deepest pools of the mind. As so often, the motive of the Jewish Bride seems first to have entered Rembrandt's consciousness as one of Raphael's "judicious pictorial inventions". A drawing in the Kramarski Collection (fig. 133) shows Isaac and Rebecca embracing, with Abimalech looking on. It is a reminiscence of a scene in Raphael's *loggie*, representing the same subject, and Rembrandt has retained the overall pose of the figures, while changing the classical garments into contemporary dress. Incidentally, the fountain in the Raphael has become a rather peculiar flowering shrub in a shallow pot—or perhaps it is still intended to be a fountain: at all events it seems to have had a symbolic importance for Rembrandt, for since the picture

Fig. 133. Rembrandt. Isaac and Rebecca. [Drawing]

has been cleaned it has reappeared. The date of the drawing is uncertain. Recognising its affinity with the Jewish Bride, students have tried
to put it as late as possible, but have not succeeded in dating it within ten
years of the picture. Viewed purely stylistically it has all the signs of an
early drawing. The long loops, the fin-like hands, the formalistic heads
can all be paralleled in drawings of the 1630's.

Of all Raphael's inventions (for although the execution of the Isaac and
Rebecca is by Giulio Romano the invention is probably Raphael's) this
is the most lyrical, and, as has often been remarked, the most Venetian;[18]
as with the Castiglione, it was probably done with Titian or Giorgione in
mind. The actual theme of loving encounter had a peculiar appeal to the
Venetian painters, perhaps because its earliest and most memorable representation in art stood at the heart of their city, the porphyry group[19] on
the corner of the Treasury of St. Mark's (fig. 136). The motive appears in
representations of the Visitation, in meetings of Jacob and Rachel, of which
there is a famous example by Palma in Dresden; and a drawing in Copenha-
gen of the meeting of Jacob and Laban (fig. 134), although personally I doubt
if it is authentic, shows that the motive was known in Rembrandt's studio.
Finally the theme of loving embrace provided a typical Venetian subject,

142

Fig. 134. Rembrandt Studio. Meeting of Jacob and Laban. [Drawing]

which seems to have been invented by Giorgione[20] and become fashionable in the 1520's, the composition known as "The Lovers." At some time in the 1660's a Venetian treatment of this subject re-awakened Rembrandt's interest in this motive which may have lain buried in his memory for almost thirty years. Indeed it is difficult not to believe that the actual picture which inspired him was the one now in Dresden (fig. 135),[21] which, up to the time of Cavalcaselle, was universally accepted as a Giorgione. Even supposing that this picture has not been cut down (and "The Lovers" pictures in the Brera and Buckingham Palace are both three-quarter length), the relation of the figures, the turn of the man's head and the placing of his hand on the woman's shoulder are all strikingly similar. But how far removed from the Jewish Bride in its effect on our feeling is this rather prosaic image of physical attachment! The

Fig. 135. Callisto da Lodi? The Lovers

Venetian lovers seem flatly, and, in the case of the lady, almost indecently material. There is little trace left of the mysterious poetry by which Giorgione transformed the world of sensation. Rembrandt not only equals Giorgione in his power of spiritualising matter, but adds a new dimension of human understanding. The relationship between the figures has a depth and subtlety which no Venetian artist, except perhaps Lorenzo Lotto, could comprehend. These are two individual souls, who nonetheless embody certain universal and enduring truths: that we need each other, that we can achieve unity only through tenderness, and that the protection of one human being by another is a solemn responsibility.

The Jewish Bride is the climax of Rembrandt's lifelong struggle to combine the particular and the universal, and he has achieved his aim in two ways; by seeing the life around him as if it were part of the Old Testament, and by relating accidents of gesture to the deep-rooted, recurring motives of mediterranean art. To argue over the picture's title is frivolous. As in all the greatest poetry, the myth, the form and the incident are one. Rembrandt saw any loving couple, long-sought and wholly devoted, as Isaac and Rebecca; and whether or not the position of their hands is that

144

of a Jewish betrothal, it is an ancient and satisfying symbol of protective union, which, in the light of Rembrandt's emotion, becomes one of the most moving areas of paint in the world.

Since de Piles, in the seventeenth century,[22] the comparison of Rembrandt and Titian has been a commonplace of criticism. I have mentioned more frequently the name of Giorgione, and it may seem far-fetched to compare this shadowy figure, with his limited and uncertain output, to an artist as abundant and many-sided as Rembrandt. But the fact is that of Rembrandt's poetic themes an astonishing number seem to have been initiated by Giorgione. Christ and the woman at the well, lovers embracing, handsome youths in shining armour, saints in wooded landscapes, moonlight scenes, portraits of men and women leaning on window-sills: we know from Michiel and other irrefutable early sources that these were the subjects introduced and perfected by Giorgione: not by Titian, but by Giorgione. So I do not think it fanciful to say that in one particular mood—call it lyrical or romantic—Rembrandt had a real affinity with Giorgione. It is a measure of his range that in the last chapter we can look at him from an almost opposite point of view.

Fig. 136. ? Fourth Century. Embracing Emperors. [Porphry]

5

Rembrandt and the Quattrocento

In the second chapter I showed how Rembrandt developed a clearer and more concentrated style by study of the classical tradition, taking his models both from the compositions of Leonardo and Raphael and from the engravings of Graeco-Roman antiques. By this means he was able to discard the rhetoric of the Baroque, which, although it appealed to his love of drama, outraged his sense of truth. But the art of the high Renaissance was also an artificial construction. Its types, gestures and draperies were contrived according to an ideal of beauty and decorum derived from classical antiquity. In using it, Rembrandt had to re-imagine it in his own terms. The great artists of the Italian Quattrocento, however, had

Fig. 137. Mantegna. The Calumny of Apelles [Drawing]

created a style which combined the nobility of classic art with a grave, unflinching naturalism. Rembrandt's real ancestors were Masaccio and Donatello.

He could not have known their work. It was not to be seen outside Italy and, even if he had gone there as a young man, he is unlikely to have visited Florence; he would have spent his time in Bologna and Rome. Nevertheless, he contrived to see a surprising quantity of quattrocento art. How did he do so? Once more our answer can proceed from a fixed point, the volume in the inventory of 1656 described as *'t Kosselijke boeck van Andre Mantagnie*—the precious book of Andrea Mantegna.

How little we can anticipate the tastes and needs of a great artist! A friend of mine who wheeled Matisse's chair round the Louvre told me that the only picture he wanted to stop in front of was Raphael's *Belle Jardinière*. He could not be persuaded to leave it. The truth is that a great artist does not want to waste time on what he can do himself, but looks for something which will extend his latent qualities and strengthen faculties which he knows to be capable of development. The mature Rembrandt needed nothing from Guercino or Terbrugghen. But he was prepared to

Fig. 138. Rembrandt. Copy of Mantegna's The Calumny of Apelles. [Drawing]

Fig. 139. Mantegna. The Calumny of Apelles (detail). [Drawing]

Fig. 140. Rembrandt. Copy of Mantegna's The Calumny of Apelles (detail). [Drawing]

Fig. 141. Rembrandt. Free copy of Mantegna's engraving of The Entombment. [Drawing]

take considerable pains in copying prints and drawings by Mantegna. An unquestioned example is his copy of a drawing representing a recorded subject of antique painting, the Calumny of Apelles. Both the original Mantegna (fig. 137) and Rembrandt copy (fig. 138) are in the British Museum, and to compare them inch by inch is a lesson in the art of looking. Art historians, who see what they expect to see, speak of Rembrandt's having rendered a plastic style as a pictorial style: but in fact Mantegna shows a more delicate sense of atmosphere (fig. 139). The way in which the reflected lights on the draperies are rendered in line and combined with a firm delineation of every form, is a miracle of technical skill. By comparison Rembrandt's execution (fig. 140) is very summary and relies on the linear convention of the sketch; and, as in the copy of Leonardo's Cenacolo, his touch is less confident than in a direct drawing from nature. It is a rehearsal, not a performance. Yet he has taken few liberties with the actual design, and the total impression is of how humbly

150

Fig. 142. Mantegna. The Entombment. [Engraving]

Rembrandt has subordinated himself to his model, even to the point of imitating Mantegna's handwriting.

In his other copy of a Mantegna (fig. 141) he has allowed himself more liberties. It is of the engraving of the Entombment (fig. 142), and looking at this noble and tragic work it is easy to see why Rembrandt was anxious to study it so closely. Only after we have compared the engraving with Rembrandt's copy do we notice how far Mantegna has followed the rhetorical conventions of both hellenistic and late gothic drapery. From almost every figure a cloak or scarf floats on an imaginary wind. These flourishes Rembrandt has cut out, even when they are inconspicuous, as in the drapery of the St. John. He has also omitted the distracted mourner with raised hands, a quotation from a Meleager sarcophagus which did not come within his experience, and this has allowed him to bring forward the head of the man carrying Our Lord so that there is a human rapport between him and the woman who is helping to carry Christ's body; she

151

looks at him with an expression of startled pity very different from the formalised grief of the Mantegna. The fainting Virgin is also younger and less anguished; and the whole mood is changed from the austere theological tragedy of Mantegna to a more human pathos: a change also implied in the alteration of the words on the sarcophagus from *Humani Generis Redemptor* to *Pio et Immortale Jesu Deo*. These masterly, and typically Rembrandtesque, alterations, leave me in little doubt that the drawing is authentic,[1] although, as in all Rembrandt's copies, parts of it are drawn without his usual certainty of touch.

Fig. 143. Rembrandt. The Triumph of Judith. [Drawing]

152

Fig. 144. Rembrandt. The Virgin and Child with a Cat. [Etching]

These are the only actual copies of Mantegna which have survived; but there are obvious echoes of Mantegna engravings in several drawings and etchings; for example, the drawing in the British Museum of the Triumph of Judith (fig. 143), which seems to me an authentic Rembrandt with the background added by a pupil, is related to the engravings of Mantegna's Triumphs.[2] The general design is based on the Senators (B. 11) and the fat trumpeters on the right are from the Elephants (B. 12). Knowing the way in which Rembrandt transformed his sources, there are no doubt others which have not yet been detected. One of them, however, is easily recognisable, and of great beauty. This is the etching of the Virgin and Child with a Cat (fig. 144) in which the pose of the principal figures is taken directly from a Mantegna engraving, B. 8 (fig. 145). Rembrandt has changed the Virgin's draperies into contemporary dress; but the most interesting feature of the paraphrase is the way in which he has taken Mantegna's isolated figure and situated it in a perspective setting, thereby making it closer to the Florentine Quattrocento than to Mantegna's antiquarian classicism. The Virgin and the cat is dated 1654, but this does

153

not prove that the "precious book" was purchased only in this decade. On the contrary, there is a drawing of the Virgin and Child in the British Museum (fig. 146) which cannot be much later than 1635, yet the hooded Virgin in profile seems to be derived from a Mantegna drawing or perhaps from one of several plaquettes executed in the workshop of Donatello (Molinier 65, 66), which may have been with Pisanello's Gian Francesco Gonzaga in Rembrandt's collection of medals (inv. no. 185)[3]. Indeed there is no reason why Rembrandt should not have bought his Mantegna book at this early date. We know that he was interested in fifteenth-century engravers like Schongauer in the 1630's, and had already begun to form his collection. Quattrocento motives were already working in his mind before he began to reform his style by copying them and studying them systematically.

The question when this Quattrocento influence first begins, leads me to consider the most puzzling and debatable of all the pictures bearing his signature, the Sacrifice of Manoah (fig. 147). It is a composition of monumental simplicity and an almost archaic stillness; and it is dated 1641. In the Dresden Gallery it hangs beside the great baroque masterpieces of the late 1630's, the Rembrandt with Saskia on his knee, and the Samson's

Fig. 145. Mantegna. Virgin and Child.
[Engraving]

Fig. 146. Rembrandt. Virgin and Child.
[Drawing]

154

Fig. 147. Attributed to Rembrandt. The Sacrifice of Manoah

Wedding of '38—and I well remember the difficulty with which, when I first saw it, I adjusted my mind to such an astonishing freak in Rembrandt's development. But I reconciled myself to it, as other students of Rembrandt had done, partly because the actual handling of the paint seemed to be that of the '40's. I have become increasingly reluctant to believe in stylistic deviations of this kind. Signatures may be added or forged, facture may be imitated; but a basic conception, both of imagery and design, comes from a painter's inner being, and must be consonant

155

with his mental and spiritual growth. With the Manoah this vague *a priori* uneasiness is supported by a quantity of concrete evidence. We know how Rembrandt conceived this subject, before the year 1640, from a drawing in Berlin[4] (fig. 148) which is unquestionably of this date. It is, of course, related to the painting in the Louvre of the Angel Departing from Tobit of '37 and has the twist and swirl of Rembrandt's baroque period. Nothing could be further in conception from the picture at Dresden. Four other drawings of the subject certainly are related to the Dresden picture. They are in an entirely different style and no competent Rembrandt scholar has ever doubted that they should be dated in the middle '50's. The magnificent drawing in the Reinhart Collection (fig. 149) is the closest to the final composition: the others show Rembrandt feeling his way towards this simple and concentrated design, and achieving on the way pictorial ideas which only he could have left undeveloped.

Why should Rembrandt have done a series of drawings in 1655 exploring a composition which he had already perfected in 1641? Scholars have put forward various explanations: that he intended to repaint, or to enlarge it, or to do another picture on the same design. The objections to

Fig. 148. Rembrandt. The Sacrifice of Manoah. [Drawing]

156

all these theories are obvious, and it seems to me that only one answer is convincing; that the Dresden Manoah was not painted in 1641 and is not by Rembrandt. I would suggest that at some time in the mid-1650's Rembrandt planned to paint a great picture of Manoah's Sacrifice. At first it was to be a large canvas with an arched top, a form which was fashionable in Dutch monumental painting of the time[5]; and as such we see it in a drawing in Stockholm (fig. 150). He then reduced it to an oblong, and may finally have conceived it as something nearer to a square, for the balance of design in the Dresden picture is so perfect that I believe it must be due to Rembrandt himself. Then, for some reason which we shall probably never know, he left the execution to a pupil, who painted, as his pupils were apt to do, in his earlier and more popular style. The signature and date remain inexplicable, unless they are spurious.

I have said that these figures have an almost archaic stillness. In fact they are obviously derived from the familiar scheme of a Quattrocento Nativity. The wife of Manoah is a Virgin kneeling in adoration of the Child, the Manoah is a Joseph. Which Nativity did Rembrandt have in

Fig. 149. Rembrandt. The Sacrifice of Manoah. [Drawing]

157

Fig. 150. Rembrandt. The Sacrifice of Manoah. [Drawing]

mind? I cannot give a definite answer, but it is worth putting forward a possibility. One of the most important early works of Leonardo da Vinci, now lost to us, but known through many studies of figures and drapery, was an Adoration of the Shepherds painted about 1478. From these drawings we know that it is reproduced fairly accurately in a picture in Va-

Fig. 151. Ferrando Llanos and Ferrando Yanez. The Adoration of the Shepherds

lencia by Leonardo's Spanish pupils Ferrando Llanos and Ferrando Yanez (fig. 151). Taken in conjunction with drapery studies in the British Museum and the Louvre, this picture suggests that some study for Leonardo's Adoration of the Shepherds more complete than any which has come down to us, was the inspiration of the Manoah.

At this point the reader may feel that I am furnishing Rembrandt's collection with an altogether improbable number of Quattrocento drawings; I will, therefore, give one or two examples of the early drawings he possessed and of the way he made use of them. The first is a drawing in

Fig. 152. Florentine circa 1450. Figure Studies. [Drawing]

Berlin (fig. 152) of three figures, including a kneeling woman and a seated man, classified by Berenson as "School of Uccello," and certainly Florentine of about the year 1440. This somewhat bleak and undernourished drawing does not look as if it would interest the painter of the Night Watch; and yet he seems to have used both these figures in two of his most carefully considered compositions, the kneeling woman in the Hundred Guilder Print and the seated man in the etching of Christ Preaching. The kneeling woman appears first in a drawing in the Louvre (fig. 153) which has been accepted by the majority of scholars[6] as a study for the "Hundred Guilder"; and taken by itself, the resemblance to the Florentine drawing might just possibly be written off as a coincidence. But when we find the other figure in the "Uccello" seated on the steps of the *Petite Tombe* (fig. 174) it is more reasonable to suppose that Rembrandt owned the drawing and was fascinated by the economical manner in which it recorded self-sufficient poses. These were the simple, unemphatic, but unforgettable, statements which he wished to make.

160

Fig. 153. Rembrandt. Christ Preaching. [Drawing]

Another group of Quattrocento drawings in his possession had a more pervasive influence. Rembrandt had always been interested in scenes comprising large groups of figures, and as late as 1637, when he had long transcended the influence of Lastman, he had made copies of such crowd scenes by his old master. In his search for a more concentrated design, the garrulous provincialism of Lastman could no longer satisfy him, and he turned for inspiration to a group of drawings in his collection, perhaps also in the "precious book" of Mantegna. Two of these drawings we can identify, since there exist copies of them made in Rembrandt's studio and also sixteenth-century Italian versions of the same drawings. One of these represents St. Mark preaching (fig. 154), a drawing formerly attributed to Rembrandt himself, although most students would now consider it a

Fig. 154. Rembrandt Studio.
St. Mark Preaching, after Carpaccio. [Drawing]

Fig. 155. Venetian, Sixteenth Century.
St. Mark Preaching, after Carpaccio. [Drawing]

162

Fig. 156. Rembrandt Studio. Alexander III and Doge Zian, after Gentile Bellini. [Drawing]

pupil's copy.[7] The Italian version of the same subject is at Chatsworth (fig. 155) and seems to be a copy of a lost Carpaccio,[8] of which presumably Rembrandt owned the original. The other copy is of a lost Gentile Bellini representing Pope Alexander III presenting a sword to Doge Zian (fig. 156).[9] Making all allowances for the unusual timidity of Rembrandt's touch when he was trying accurately to reproduce an Italian model, I do not think the drawing in the Albertina is from his hand, although it is certainly from his studio and may well be a copy of *his* copy. Our only other record of the original is a sixteenth-century copy in the British Museum. This cannot have been the drawing which belonged to Rembrandt, and I think it probable that, as with the Polidoro Caravaggio Entombment (fig. 64), he owned a magnificent original now lost to us.

If, as seems possible, the "precious book" of Andrea Mantegna was an album of North Italian and Venetian drawings put together in the sixteenth century, Rembrandt knew other examples of Carpaccio and Bellini, in addition to those which have chanced to survive, and it is not

Fig. 157. Carpaccio. Two Groups of Ecclesiastics. [Drawing]

difficult to account for their influence on his style. They influenced him in two ways. First, they showed him how to group figures on a single plane in such a way as to achieve variety, dignity and decorative effect. This type of composition, perfected by Masaccio in the Carmine and Donatello in his reliefs in the Santo at Padua, had, by the end of the century, become part of the Quattrocento tradition of design. It was common form in the Venice of the Bellinis no less than in the Florence of Ghirlandaio. A Carpaccio drawing (fig. 157) formerly in the Harewood Collection is a typical example, and is so like certain Rembrandts, both in the disposition of the figures and in the rectangular shapes by which they are indicated, that one is tempted to believe it was once in "the precious book". Secondly, these drawings influenced Rembrandt's use of the pen. The deliberate outlines, with a minimum of shadow, far removed from Rembrandt's earlier drawing technique, appear in a series of drawings done between the years 1652 and 1656. An example is the Stockholm version of Christ

164

Fig. 158. Rembrandt. Homer Reciting. [Drawing]

Fig. 159. Rembrandt. Manoah's Sacrifice. [Drawing]

and the Adulteress, which I discuss later (fig. 170), and an even more valuable instance, because it is dated 1652, is the famous drawing of Homer Reciting (fig. 158) which seems to be Rembrandt's earliest essay in the Carpaccio style. The balance and character of the line, and the way of indicating heads and hands, are so alike that one might well suspect the influence of Carpaccio, even were there not positive evidence to support it.

While on the subject of Rembrandt's drawing technique in these years, I may add that the influence of Carpaccio's bold linear style seems to run parallel with that of Mantegna's more delicate penmanship and fine shading. The drawing in the Lugt Collection of the angel departing from Manoah (fig. 159)—a version of the subject independent of the group discussed earlier—which must be a little later than the Homer drawing of 1652, is in a style similar to the Mantegna copies. The Persian costume of Manoah in this drawing shows that it is also of about the same date as the strangest of all Rembrandt's sources of inspiration, a group of Mogul miniatures (fig. 160) of which he is known to have made at least twenty-eight copies.[10] No doubt one reason for copying them was the belief that

166

Fig. 160. Rembrandt. Copy of Mogul miniature. [Drawing]

they would give him information about the people of the East (even about
their foot-wear), which he took to be a single, unchanging territory, once
inhabited by the dramatis personae of the Old Testament. But we cannot
doubt that an even stronger impulse was his reaction against the com-
plexities of baroque design, which had already led him to seek for parallelism and simplicity in classical reliefs and in Quattrocento grouping. The
miniatures he copied, many of which are now in the Schönbrunn Palace,
are in fact second-rate examples of almost contemporary Mogul painting, but he found in them a mastery of the profile rooted in the long tradition of Middle-Eastern art. The Jews of the captivity, if they had looked
at the forbidden images of their conquerors, would have seen figures in

167

Fig. 161. Rembrandt. The Three Crosses (1653). [Etching]

this profile style, so in a sense Rembrandt was right in thinking that these miniatures were some sort of evidence of how people of biblical times had appeared to one another. Indeed, as we study these extraordinary recreations of the East, we begin to feel that for Rembrandt the profile pose was not simply a useful element of design. Did he not feel that it gave to an image a sort of magic, or at least a timelessness, placing it outside the flux of action?

This feeling of the magical remoteness of the profile is confirmed by one of the most haunting of all Rembrandt's quotations from the Quattrocento. It occurs in the second version (fourth state) of his great etching the Three Crosses. In the first version (fig. 161), executed in 1653, the

168

Fig. 162. Rembrandt. The Three Crosses (circa 1661). [Etching]

Cross rises above a world of uncertainty and distress. For almost the first
time since the Night Watch, Rembrandt's sense of space is agitated and
contradictory. The tautest element in the design is the relationship of Our
Lord and the kneeling centurion, who is in fact taken from a Raphaelesque engraving.[11] The plate contains marvellous details—the Düreresque
knight in armour to the left, the cavernous sepulchre in the bottom right
hand corner; but one can understand why Rembrandt felt the need to
re-work it. Recent scholars believe that he did so at least seven years later
and we may agree that the fourth state (fig. 162) has the character of such
recklessly personal works as the Conspiracy of Claudius Civilis. It is both

169

Fig. 163. Pisanello. Portrait of Gian Francesco Gonzaga. [Lead]

abstract and passionate; the fierce geometric framework encloses a micro-cosm of mysterious vitality. The central human figure of the earlier state, the Raphaelesque centurion, has almost vanished and behind his shadow there rises a man on horse-back, whose weird profile is obviously derived from Pisanello's medal of Gian Francesco Gonzaga (fig. 163). By what stroke of inspiration did Rembrandt see this bizarre figure as adding something to the mystery of a darkened world? Did he feel in Pisanello's perfectly calculated profile a detachment which he could use as a symbol of loneliness (fig. 164)? Did he feel, as in the Claudius Civilis, that some touch of the grotesque would heighten our feeling of the in-comprehensible? This enormous hat[12] seems to have grown in the night like a giant toadstool. It belongs to the non-human order; and yet the chinless head below it is human and touching in its feeling of resignation. And to give it greater poignancy, Rembrandt has adumbrated behind this passive, unclassical image one of the great symbols of classical energy, the horse-tamer of the Quirinal. Once more he makes use of allusions and analogies which cannot be accounted for by coincidence, and argues a deep understanding of the mechanism of the unconscious.

170

Fig. 164. Rembrandt. The Three Crosses (detail). [Etching]

Just as critics of Shakespeare, following Milton's lead, used to speak of him as "warbling his native woodnotes wild", and ignored the counterpoint of classical allusion in *King Lear*, so Rembrandt scholars for long pretended that Rembrandt addressed us directly, with artless simplicity; perhaps because the myth of the inspired simpleton is the only way in which we can preserve our *amour propre*, by shielding ourselves from the realisation that genius involves mental faculties of an altogether different order from our own.

Rembrandt's interest in profiles and parallelism was accompanied by the study of another element in fifteenth-century design: the arrangement of figures in space on a geometric basis, known as perspective. This scheme for constructing on a flat surface a measurable and manageable space was invented in the early years of the fifteenth century by the architect Brunelleschi, and received its first theoretical statement in Leon Battista Alberti's *Della Pittura* in 1435. It was a rectilinear system. Not only did it assume the fact that light travels to the eye in a straight line, but it accepted the convenient fiction that transversals are straight and parallel with the pic-

171

ture plane; and it therefore led to compositions based on rectangles, with all subsidiary shapes conforming to the same rules. The baroque designers, with their love of curves, overlapping form and continuous movement, had abandoned the compositional elements of perspective. They did not abandon the science: books on perspective continued to appear in the late sixteenth and seventeenth centuries, and grew more elaborately theoretical. But by emphasising a narrow convergence on the vanishing point and often placing it outside the frame, they used the mechanism of reason to create a setting for the irrational. We may call this mannerist, as opposed to Quattrocento, perspective.

Rembrandt certainly knew these treatises in his youth, and associated them with the type of baroque composition to which these diagrams were related. In several early drawings, for example that of a painter in his studio (Ben. 390), perspective lines are sketchily indicated, and show the vanishing point outside the frame, or at the extreme edge. In the Night Watch, with its basically Raphaelesque architecture, he uses central perspective as the best means of controlling such a large, crowded composition; then, in the late 1640's, he began to think of perspective not as a trick or a form of display, but as a means of telling the truth more directly, and giving to his compositions the persuasive character of a rational proposition. This involved abandoning mannerist or baroque perspective, with its off-centre vanishing point, and returning to Quattrocento perspective, where the vanishing point is in the centre of the picture. There was a renewed interest in central perspective about the year 1645, of which the most dogmatic example is Poussin's Landscape with a Roman Road (1648). Poussin's compositions were known in Rembrandt's studio (see p. 213 n. 13), and no doubt Rembrandt learnt from them more than we can recognise.[13] However, I think it probable that he would have arrived at the same point independently, and, in fact, his inspiration and information do not seem to have been drawn from contemporary sources, but from prints and drawing of the Renaissance. The inventory lists (no. 273) Dürer's book on proportion; and, more important, we know that he owned a number of Dürer's woodcuts of the Passion and the Life of the Virgin. It is of these immaculate interiors, in which space is, so to say, argued step by step, that we think when we follow Rembrandt's use of perspective in the early 1650's.

172

Fig. 165. Rembrandt. Jews in the Synagogue. [Etching]

The precise date at which Rembrandt adopted Quattrocento perspective and derived from it a new form of design raises a problem which is cardinal to the whole history of Dutch painting in the 1650's. From 1655 to 1660 the finest works of Dutch genre painting were composed on a strict scheme of box-perspective and dominated by rectangular design. To some extent this may reflect the fashion for classicism which I have just mentioned. But since, in the 1640's, almost every promising Dutch painter, including those who were to become masters of perspective like Carel Fabritius and Hoogstraten, had graduated in Rembrandt's studio, it is reasonable to suppose that they were first influenced by experiments and tendencies current in that forcing-house of talent. In Rembrandt's own work the earliest dated example—there are a few undated drawings which may be a year or two earlier[14]—is a small etching of Jews in a synagogue of 1648 (fig.165), where the vertical and horizontal lines of the composition are related to the rectangular masonry.[15] In spite of its scale and quasi-satirical intention,[16] the small plate has a stillness and monumentality lacking in his earlier compositions; and I question if this kind of classical design can be found anywhere in Dutch art before this date. Rembrandt's pupils were amazingly precocious, but even Nicholas Maes could not

Fig. 166. Rembrandt. Christ among the Doctors. [Drawing]

Fig. 167. Rembrandt. Christ among the Doctors (1652) [Etching]

174

Fig. 168. Rembrandt. Christ among the Doctors (1654) [Etching]

have invented a new type of interior at the age of fourteen.[17] Nevertheless it must be admitted that there is a gap in the dated examples of Rembrandt's classical perspective between the Jews in a synagogue of 1648 and the Virgin with a Cat of 1654 (fig. 144); and we can follow his development of this kind of composition only in drawings, the dates of which must often be conjectural. An example is a drawing in the Louvre of Christ among the Doctors (fig. 166) which students of Rembrandt have dated with exceptional unanimity about the year 1652. It is an extreme example of the use of Quattrocento perspective; the placing of the figures in their box is almost like an Albertian demonstration, and it may be no coincidence that Alberti's *Della Pittura* was printed as an appendix to Leonardo's *Trattato* in 1651. The man leaning forward on the right, by his likeness to a figure in Holbein, supports my suggestion that Rembrandt's use of perspective was partly inspired by early sixteenth-century German woodcuts. In 1652 Rembrandt had sketched another version of the scene on an etching plate (fig. 167). Although this print is full of life and psychological insight, the drawing shows a great advance in clarity and there

175

can be little doubt that it is later. The perspective setting not only creates logical space, but actually increases our sense of dramatic truth, by isolating the small, magisterial figure of Christ, and using the man looking down from the gallery to emphasise his diminutive stature. However, Rembrandt seems to have felt that this composition was too dogmatic and symmetrical for an etching, so when, in 1654, he finally committed the subject to a copper plate it is treated with a curious informality (fig. 168). The doctors are rustics, like shepherds in an Adoration, and the gallery on the right, all that remains of the Louvre drawing, might be a manger. But the Christ is older and more serious and we recognise that Rembrandt's theme was the sudden revelation of His intellectual authority. This is confirmed by a companion etching of Christ returning home with his parents (Munz 230), who, humble and thoughtful, seem for the first time to be aware of their son's extraordinary powers.

How Rembrandt concealed, in the interests of a more direct appeal to our feelings, his learning and intellectual power is beautifully shown in another work of 1654, the etching known as The Virgin and Child with a Cat (fig. 144). I have already pointed out how the Virgin, seated on the ground, and leaning forward till her cheek touches her infant's face, is derived from an engraving by Mantegna. Rembrandt takes this ancient traditional pose and gives it a new reality. To begin with he places it in a modest interior, which, both by its perspective scheme and by the large area of window parallel with the picture plane, anticipates the settings of De Hooch and Vermeer. But as usual with Rembrandt at this date, his conception of the subject goes far beyond naturalism and reveals, to an attentive eye, layer upon layer of imaginative deposit. This is a picture of an ordinary man brooding on his awareness of divinity. Silently and unperceived, he looks in and sees these two familiar beings transformed. The pose of the Mantegna, precisely because it was outside Rembrandt's ordinary range of perception, has the quality of a magic symbol; and for this reason has been followed more closely than most of Rembrandt's other derivations. By a stroke of genius the geometrical design and the perspective scheme are combined to bring together the two planes of reality; for the central panel of the window acts as a halo to the Virgin, but the vanishing point of the perspective, clearly indicated by the floor boards, is St. Joseph's head. Rembrandt may seem to be at the opposite

176

Fig. 169. Rembrandt. The Adulteress Brought Before Christ. [Drawing]

pole to Piero della Francesca, but perhaps Piero is the only other painter who has used perspective in this way to express a religious idea.

This feeling, which we have already seen in his treatment of Christ among the Doctors, that a display of pictorial learning and architectonics might actually diminish the dramatic impact of the scene, was never far from Rembrandt's mind, and is so important a factor in his art that I will give one more example. In a drawing in Rotterdam of the Adulteress brought before Christ (fig. 169) he has constructed a space almost as elaborate as the background of a Paul Veronese. The figures are admirably disposed, and by the standards of Italian painting the episode is as dramatic as one could wish. Yet Rembrandt felt that the verses of St. John's Gospel, which must have touched him personally, for in 1654 Hendrickje had appeared three times before the Church Council to be admonished for her relationship with Rembrandt, should be illustrated with greater

Fig. 170. Rembrandt. Christ and the Adulteress. [Drawing]

simplicity and concentration. So in the drawing in Stockholm (fig. 170) he reduced the scene to its essentials, placed the figures parallel with the picture plane and indicated them with the barest outlines. I have already mentioned this drawing as a particularly clear example of a type of penmanship which seems to derive from the Venetian Quattrocento, imitated from actual examples by Gentile Bellini and Carpaccio. There is a possibility that the composition itself has the same origin. This unusual subject[18] occurs in an early painting by Jacopo Bassano (fig. 171) which still hangs in the municipal museum of his native city. Comparison with Rembrandt's drawing shows unmistakable similarities in the arrangement of the principal figures: the kneeling Christ, the adulteress standing in isolation, the figure to the right indicating her, the chief figure to the left turned away from us. Rembrandt cannot have known the Bassano, which is an early work and was never engraved; and a possible ex-

178

Fig. 171. Jacopo Bassano. Christ and the Adulteress

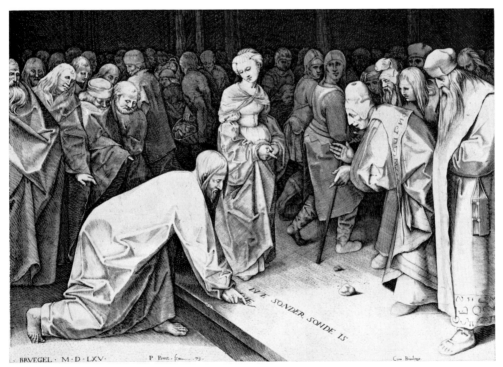

Fig. 172. Pieter Breughel. Christ and the Adulteress. [Engraving]

planation of these similarities would seem to be that both designs go back to the same original, perhaps a Carpaccio or a Gentile Bellini. This would account both for the archaic style of the Bassano, almost unique in his work, and for the unusually spare and linear technique of the Stockholm drawing. It is characteristic of Rembrandt that, having derived his compositions from a Venetian source, he should have allowed a print by Breughel (Bastelaer no. 111) to furnish his imagination with a more vivid image of Christ writing on the ground (fig. 172). Needless to say, these sources of inspiration do not prevent his drawing from being the quintessence of Rembrandt in its grasp of a human situation. The *affectuum vivacitas*, once elaborated into something approaching caricature, is now concealed in these dots and scribbles that express intense sympathy through a severe shortland.

The change in Rembrandt's style from cursive, overlapping forms to rectangular cubic forms (of which the adulteress's skirt in the Stockholm drawing is such a clear example) coincided with his interest in perspective, and may be, to some extent, dependent on it, since Albertian perspective imposes a rectilinear pattern on the composition which can extend, as in the case of Uccello, from the whole to the parts. However, in all questions of this kind, it is difficult to distinguish between cause and effect. From about 1650 till almost the end of his life Rembrandt's love of rectilinear forms seems to have been innate, a kind of physical necessity perceptible in his actual brush strokes, and transforming his whole mode of vision, even in his portraits (fig. 173). This development can be closely paralleled in the work of Cézanne. He, too, started with the feeling that violent emotions must be expressed by curvilinear rhythms, heavily agitated and ungraceful; and he, too, in middle life not only compressed his sensations into cubes, but changed his facture from cursive to rectangular strokes of the brush. In his case the study of perspective played no part; in fact, as has been frequently observed, his concept of space was a revolt against academic perspective. In books on both Rembrandt and Cézanne this period in their development is usually referred to as classical, but it is difficult to find any justification for applying this hard-worked word to a rectilinear system of design. In so far as the word classical is related to the art of Graeco-Roman antiquity, it should be indicative of a smooth and continuous modelling, for this was an essential part of the Greek ideal of

Fig. 173. Rembrandt. Self-portrait

Fig. 174. Rembrandt. Christ Preaching the Remission of Sins. [Etching]

beauty, and was re-affirmed by Raphael and Leonardo. In all but the most skilful hands smoothness is enervating, and at various periods artists have recognised that a convex surface can affect us more vividly if it is rendered as a series of facets or planes; the splitting up of an apparent continuum often permits a firmer grasp of its real construction. There are examples of this procedure in French mediaeval sculpture and in Giovanni Pisano; but the most striking instances are to be found in the work of fifteenth-century Florentines. The shoulders of Pollaiuolo's Antaeus are as squarely and vigorously facetted as a Cézanne; and in this Pollaiuolo was no doubt following the lead of Donatello, who, although he could achieve the apparent smoothness of the David, was always thinking in terms of a vigorous progression of planes. Thus Rembrandt's need to simplify all forms into cubes or rectangles with a clear structural relationship to each other, was connected with Quattrocento art in a way which cannot be accounted

182

for by study and imitation, but derives from a profound similarity of outlook. It supports, and is perhaps the expression of, a parallel imagery, and reflects a similar scale of human values.

As an example of how all these characteristics may be drawn together in a single work, let us consider the etching known as the *Petite Tombe* (fig. 174). It represents Christ preaching the remission of sins, an event which does not occur in the Gospels, but which played an important part in Mennonite doctrine. As so often with unusual subjects, Rembrandt found an iconographical precedent in the work of a mannerist illustrator, an engraving by Marten de Vos entitled *Remissionem Peccatorum* (fig. 175). But although there is unmistakable evidence that he knew this print, it is at the opposite pole to Rembrandt's etching, both in imagery and style. The poses, the types, and the setting of the Marten de Vos all look artificial and unreal; whereas the Rembrandt appears to be completely natural. Like the Bathsheba, it seems to have the simplicity of a personal experience; and yet when we study its origins, we find that it is rooted in the central tradition of mediterranean painting.

The first foreshadowing of the composition appears in the drawing in the Six family album (which I mentioned on p. 166 as an example of Car-

Fig. 175. Marten de Vos.
Remissionem Peccatorum. [Engraving]

183

Fig. 176. Marcantonio after Raphael. Parnassus. [Engraving]

paccio's influence) where Rembrandt, in deference to the cultivated taste of his friend, has depicted a classical subject, Homer reciting his verses (fig. 158). In content and composition the Six drawing is clearly inspired by the Homer in Marcantonio's print of Raphael's Parnassus (fig. 176), and a comparison between them shows how unpredictably Rembrandt remembered and recombined the elements in his models. The muses in profile are memorable and we are not surprised to find them repeated, but the muse peering round a tree is the most obscure figure in the whole of Marcantonio's print; yet she reappears on the extreme right of Rembrandt's drawing. From this classical exercise Rembrandt wished to use again the idea of the draped central figure standing on a bank or parapet, raising his head, with two listeners seated on either side, and another on a lower plane seen from behind. But at the back of his mind was another great design of a figure speaking from a rostrum, with listeners gathered

184

below, Raphael's tapestry cartoon of St. Paul Preaching at Ephesus (fig. 177). This memory led him to use the Homer figure in isolation, adapted to a horizontal frame, with a calm intersection of horizontals and verticals. He has remembered some of the figures in Raphael's cartoon, the man on the right leaning forward, whom he had already used[19] in the etching of Christ Presented to the People (fig. 25), the man on the left with his hand on his chin and the fat man with a hooded cape beside him,[20] whom Rembrandt has placed on a higher step. The St. Paul could not be accommodated to his basic idea of a frontal figure, but Rembrandt discovered in another Raphael design a sublime gesture of all-inclusive forgiveness and benediction, the gesture of the Christ in the *Disputa;* only, instead of embracing in it the Saints, Apostles and Fathers of the Church, it is bestowed on sinners, that is to say on ordinary people like ourselves. For, when we have acknowledged Rembrandt's debt to Raphael, what a

Fig. 177. Raphael. St. Paul Preaching at Ephesus. [Tempera on paper]

185

difference exists between them, a difference that can be expressed in two words: common humanity. Raphael, dazzled by the perfection of antique art, felt bound to reform all his types, so that each, according to his age and character, is an ideal human specimen. In the cartoon they listen to St. Paul with the demonstrative attention of actors, anxious to justify their places in the cast. Turn back to Rembrandt's etching and how far we are from this bodily prosperity, this outward-turning energy. Christ's hearers are a very mixed lot, some thoughtful, some half-amused, some only concerned with keeping warm or keeping awake. And yet this marvellous feat of observation is without the vulgar anarchy of realism. These individuals are united, not only by a hidden mastery of design, but by Rembrandt's all-embracing, all-forgiving, love of his fellow men.

This world which Rembrandt created in his later years is not entirely without precedent in European art. On the contrary, the expression of moral and religious feeling through plain, unidealised human beings is a long tradition going back, perhaps, to the late antique concept of the stoic philosopher. There is something curiously apposite in the fact that the favourite subject of Rembrandt's early years was that of a philosopher in meditation. In such a work of the late second century as the group of philosophers with a young pupil, now in the Museo delle Terme, we are first aware of a Rembrandtesque feeling in classic art. This embodiment of moral and spiritual grandeur, independent of physical perfection, was one of the great achievements of the Middle Ages. The saints and confessors of Chartres are ordinary men, rough, raw-boned and unshaven; yet we are in no doubt about their faith, dignity and strength of purpose, any more than we are about the prophets and apostles in Rembrandt's drawings. This was the quality which Donatello and Masaccio combined with classic design, and so created what (in spite of its Pagan and Judaic origin) I may call the tradition of Christian humanism. Comparisons of this kind often rest on accident or coincidence, but I think that a likeness between Rembrandt's drawings and Donatello's marble relief of the Ascension in the Victoria and Albert Museum (fig. 178) is fundamental and depends on the same approach to humanity and to the problem of form. In such a figure as the kneeling Virgin, Donatello has concentrated his knowledge of the movements which reveal emotion into a shape reduced to its essence, like some weather-worn stone. If, as

Fig. 178. Donatello. The Ascension (detail). [Marble]

seems probable, this relief comes from the altar of the Brancacci Chapel,[21] there would have been on either side of it the frescoes in which Masaccio had imagined a similar world of convinced and upright men. The scenes in which St. Peter and St. John perform their acts of mercy (fig. 179) are at the furthest remove from the sweeping eloquence of Baroque design, and the reason lies in a different human approach. Masaccio, in reading the Acts of the Apostles, has been moved by the humanity of the early Christian church, and his St. Peter seems charged with a noble compassion for the humble believers on whom his shadow falls. The same feeling of a compassion so intense that it has the power of healing, inspired the greatest of Rembrandt's later works, the Prodigal Son (fig. 180) in the Hermitage, and has produced a similar design. In both we feel that any emphatic gesture, any curve or twist or lively diagonal, might disturb the stillness in which miracles are performed. And within this austere framework, Rembrandt's group of father and son has itself the completeness of some ancient symbol. Just as the only real precedent of the Polish Rider is the gothic horseman at Bamberg, which Rembrandt had never seen, so this group reminds us of one of the great carvings of the Middle Ages, the Abraham and Isaac at Chartres. Like the mediaeval sculptor Rembrandt has expressed the unity of father and

187

son by compressing them into a single block; and he has added another ancient image, the son's head enclosed in the diamond of the father's arms, a motive that appears in one of the earliest surviving representations of the Virgin and Child an early Christian ivory of the Adoration (fig. 181).

What are we to make of these analogies with great works of art which Rembrandt can never have seen and cannot even have known by one of those 'carriers', copies or crude reminiscences, by which the germ of a formal idea is communicated down the centuries to those who are ready to receive it? They are too close and too frequent to be dismissed as mere coincidence; yet any alternative explanation leads us beyond the borders of concrete evidence and the ordinary process of reason. No doubt we take this step every time we use the word 'inspiration'; but we have grown accustomed to a thoughtless usage, and realise the seriousness of our commitment only when the evidence of inspiration takes so concrete

Fig. 179. Masaccio. St. Peter's Shadow Healing the Sick
[Fresco]

188

Fig. 180. Rembrandt. The Return of the Prodigal Son

a form. It is this inspired sense of kinship with the great art of the past which makes Rembrandt's borrowings from Raphael, Mantegna and the Venetians something entirely different from mere imitation, and seems to justify an examination of sources that would otherwise be pedantic. The creative process will always remain mysterious; but with these clear indications to guide us we may, perhaps, penetrate a little way towards the centre of this mystery.

Fig. 181. Early Christian.
Adoration of the Magi. [Ivory]

190

The 1656 Inventory of Rembrandt's Possessions

A Short List of Chief Books and Articles Used

Notes

Index

The 1656 Inventory of Rembrandt's Possessions

The original is in the state archives of Amsterdam. An English translation was published in 1836 in Smith's *Catalogue Raisonné*, Vol VII, p. XLI; but this was only an incomplete selection, and contained many mistakes. The complete original text was first printed in 1841 by J. Immerzeel *Lofrede op Rembrandt*. A French translation, almost complete and fairly accurate, was included in Charles Blanc's *l'Oeuvre de Rembrandt*, 1853, p. 17. The text commonly used is that printed in Hofstede de Groot, *Urkunde uber Rembrandt*, 1906, p. 190. In this a few of the more obscure Dutch words are translated into German, and there are somewhat misleading references to Bode's catalogue. The same text (with the same words translated from German into English) is printed in Bode's *Complete Work of Rembrandt*, Vol VIII, p. 235. No up-to-date critical edition of the inventory exists. It would require a great range of specialised knowledge and would perhaps be best undertaken by some institution. I have added only a few notes on the artists represented in Rembrandt's collection and other obvious matters. Some of the Dutch words used to describe Rembrandt's possessions have long ago passed out of currency and are not to be found in any dictionary of the Dutch language, even Vervijs and Verdam, *Middle Nederlandsch Woordenboek*. In such cases I have printed the original word, with what seems to be the most plausible guess at an English equivalent.

Inventory of the Paintings, Furniture and other Effects contained in the house of Rembrandt van Rijn Living in the Breestreet by the St. Anthony Water-Gate

1. One small picture of Adrian Brouwer, representing a pastrycook.
2. One ditto of gamblers by the same Brouwer.
3. One ditto of a woman and child by Rembrandt van Rijn.
4. One painter's studio by the same Brouwer.

1. Adrian Brouwer, 1605–1638. Rembrandt evidently admired his scenes of 'low life' and owned seven examples of his work and a book of his drawings.

5. One rich spread of food [*vette Kokenti*] by the same Brouwer.

6. One head in plaster.

7. Two naked children in plaster.

8. One sleeping child in plaster.

9. One *poviesie* shoe.

10. One small landscape by Rembrandt.

11. Another landscape by the same.

12. One small standing figure by the same.

13. One Nativity by Jan Lievens.

14. One St. Jerome by Rembrandt.

15. One small painting of hares by the same.

16. One small painting of a hog by the same.

17. One small landscape by Hercules Seghers.

18. One landscape by Jan Lievens.

19. Another by the same.

20. One small landscape by Rembrandt.

21. One lion hunt by the same.

22. One moonlight scene by Jan Lievens.

23. One head by Rembrandt.

24. One head by the same.

25. One still life retouched by Rembrandt.

5. The subject of a table laden with food was fashionable in Flemish art in the first quarter of the seventeenth century.

9. The word *poriesie* or *poviesie* has defeated Dutch scholars.

13. Jan Lievens, 1607–1674. He was closely associated with Rembrandt up to the year 1631; later he went to Antwerp and developed an independent and more fashionable style. Rembrandt owned seven of his works and a scrap-book with drawings by Lievens and Bol.

17. Hercules Seghers, 1589–1633. One of the most individual and imaginative of Dutch artists of the early 17th century, more appreciated by his fellow painters than by collectors. Chiefly known by his small horizontal landscapes, which have often been enlarged to make them a conventional proportion. Rembrandt owned eight of these landscapes, and was undoubtedly influenced by them. His etchings, of almost incredible originality, were certainly known to Rembrandt as he re-worked the actual plate of Seghers' Tobias and the Angel to make his etching of the Flight into Egypt. Munz, 216.

18. 19. 22. Landscapes by Lievens in Berlin, no. 816, National Gallery, London, no. 22, and in the National Gallery of Scotland, Edinburgh.

25. A still life with books in the Rijksmuseum, could well be in part by Rembrandt, only in that case the books, by Rembrandt, seem to have then done first, and the other objects added by Jan Jansz. den Uyl.

194

26. One soldier in armour by the same.

27. One *vanitas* retouched by Rembrandt.

28. One of the same, with a sceptre, retouched.

29. One seascape completed by Hendrick Antonisz.

30. Four Spanish chairs with Russian leather.

31. Two Spanish chairs with black seats.

32. One pinewood *soldertie* [stand?]

In the Sydel Caemer [ante-chamber]

33. One painting of the Samaritan retouched by Rembrandt.

34. One [painting of the] Rich Man by Palma Vecchio, of which Pieter de la Tombe owns a half share.

35. One backyard by Rembrandt.

36. Two greyhounds from the life by the same.

37. One large [painting of the] Descent from the Cross with a handsome gold frame, by the same.

38. One Raising of Lazarus, by the same.

39. One courtesan doing her hair, by the same.

40. One wooded landscape, by Hercules Seghers.

41. One Tobias by Lastman.

42. One raising of Lazarus by Jan Lievens.

43. One small mountain landscape by Rembrandt.

44. One landscape by Govaert Jansz.

27. A *vanitas* was a type of still life, usually containing a skull, hour-glass and other emblems of mortality. The Leyden school specialised in this genre. c.f. Ingvar Bergstrom, *Hollandskt Stillebenmaleri*, 1947, pp. 162–165.

29. Hendrick Anthonissen, c. 1605–1656, Amsterdam painter, specialising in marine subjects in the style of his brother-in-law Jan Porcellis, see no. 47.

30. Dives and Lazarus. No painting of this subject by Palma Vecchio is known; perhaps Rembrandt owned a version of the famous Dives and Lazarus by Bonifazio da Pietati in the Venice Academy, 291. Pieter de la Tombe was an art dealer with whom Rembrandt also owned a half share of no. 109. He dealt in Rembrandt etchings, and it is from him, not from the tomb-like podium, that the etching of Christ Preaching (fig. 174) took its old title the *Petite Tombe*.

37. Probably the picture in the Hermitage, dated 1634. H. de G., 135.

38. Possibly the picture in the Gates Collection, New York. H. de G., 107.

39. Possibly the picture in the Hermitage, no, 817, dated 1654. H. de G., 309.

44. Govaert Jansz, 1578–1619, Dutch landscape painter.

45. Two heads by Rembrandt.

46. One grisaille by Jan Lievens.

47. Two grisailles by Porcellis.

48. One head by Rembrandt.

49. One ditto by Brouwer.

50. One view of the dunes by Porcellis.

51. One smaller ditto by the same.

52. One small painting of a hermit by Jan Lievens.

53. Two small heads by Lucas van Valckenburgh.

54. One small camp or stockade on fire [*brandent leger*] by old Bassano.

55. One quack salesman after Brouwer.

56. Two heads by Jan Pynas.

57. One perspective by Lucas van Leyden.

58. One priest after Jan Lievens.

59. One small study of a model by Rembrandt.

60. One small picture of a herdsman and animals by the same.

61. One drawing by the same.

62. One scourging of Christ by the same.

63. One grisaille by Porcellis.

64. One grisaille by Simon de Vlieger.

65. One small landscape by Rembrandt.

66. One head painted from life by Rembrandt.

67. One head by Raphael of Urbino.

68. Some horses painted from nature by Rembrandt.

69. One landscape painted from nature by the same.

70. Some small houses by Hercules Seghers.

47. Jan Porcellis or Percellis, c. 1584–1619. Marine painter and etcher born in Ghent, active in Rotterdam and Haarlem. Rembrandt evidently liked marine subjects as he owned four by Porcellis and two by Vlieger.

53. Lucas van Valckenburgh, c. 1530–1622 Flemish genre painter.

54. *leger* means an encampment, but this was probably a fire in a stockade with panicking animals and may have inspired Rembrandt's etching of the Annunciation to the Shepherds. Munz no. 199.

56. Jan Pynas, 1583–1631, a Haarlem painter who was in Rome with Elsheimer and Lastman, and whose drawings are sometimes claimed as an influence on Rembrandt.

57. Inventoried among the pictures, so presumably a painting. The wood and copper engravings of Lucas van Leyden are listed below, 193 and 198.

64. Simon de Vlieger, 1600–1633, Dutch marine painter and etcher.

71. One Juno by Pynas.
72. One mirror in an ebony frame.
73. One ebony frame.
74. One marble wine cooler.
75. One walnut table with a *tournai* cover.
76. Seven Spanish chairs with green velvet seats.

In the Room behind the Sydel Caemer

77. One picture of Jephta.
78. One Virgin and Child by Rembrandt.
79. One sketch of the Crucifixion by the same.
80. One naked woman by the same.
81. One copy after Anibale Carracci.
82. Two half-lengths by Brouwer.
83. Another copy after Anibale Carracci.
84. One small seascape by Porcellis.
85. One head of an old man by van Eyck.
86. One portrait of a dead man by Abraham Vinck.
87. One Resurrection of the Dead by Aertie van Leyden.
88. One sketch by Rembrandt.
89. One copy of a sketch by Rembrandt.
90. Two heads from the life by Rembrandt.
91. The Consecration of Solomon's temple by the same.
92. The Circumcision of Christ, copy after Rembrandt.
93. Two small landscapes by Hercules Seghers.
94. One gilt frame.
95. One small oak table.
96. Four *kaert schilden* [? cardboard shades].

86. Abraham Vinck, c. 1580–1621. A German painter, working in Amsterdam. In the early seventeenth century there was a fashion for painting likenesses immediately after death; e.g. a Marc Geehraerts in the Kroller-Muller Collection or the picture of John Tradescant the Elder on his deathbed ascribed to de Critz, in the Ashmolean Museum, Oxford. Poole *Catologue of Portraits*, 1912, fol I, p. 171, no. 415. c.f. also No. 188 and 295.
87. Aert Claesz, known as Aert van Leyden, c. 1498–1564, painted in the style of Heemskerk. Lived and died in Leyden.
96. Probably transparent shades to give a diffused light for etching.

97. One oak chest.

98. Four ordinary chairs.

99. Four green chair cushions.

100. One copper kettle.

101. One wardrobe.

In the Room behind the Saloon

102. One small wooded landscape by an unknown master.

103. One head of an old man by Rembrandt.

104. One large landscape by Hercules Seghers.

105. One head of a woman by Rembrandt.

106. One Unification of the Country by the same.

107. One view of a village by Govaert Jansz.

108. One small picture of an ox, painted from life, by Rembrandt.

109. One large painting of the Samaritan Woman by Giorgione, of which a half share belongs to Pieter la Tombe.

110. Three antique statues.

111. One sketch of the Entombment of Christ by Rembrandt.

112. One boat of St. Peter by Aertie van Leyden.

113. One Christ rising from the tomb by Rembrandt.

114. One image of the Virgin by Raphael of Urbino.

115. One head of Christ by Rembrandt.

116. One small winter landscape by Grimmer.

117. The Crucifixion of Christ by Lelio da Novellara.

118. Head of Christ by Rembrandt.

119. One ox by Lastman.

104. The only surviving *large* landscape by Hercules Seghers is in the Uffizi. no. 1303.

106. Rembrandt's painting of the Unification of the Netherlands, dated 1641 is now in the Boymans Museum, Rotterdam, no. 238.

109. For speculations as to the identity of the picture see p. 114.

111. Possibly the picture in the Hunterian Collection, University of Glasgow. H. de G. no. 139.

115. Rembrandt painted a number of heads of Christ, listed in H. de G., nos. 158–167.

116. Abel Grimmer, active Antwerp 1592–1619. There are three other Grimmers, but Abel is the most likely to have painted a 'small winter landscape.'

117. Lelio Orsi da Novellara, 1511–1586. The presence of this picture in Rembrandt's collection confirms his interest in the imaginative elements of mannerism.

120. One *vanitas* retouched by Rembrandt.

121. One *Ecce Homo* in grisaille by Rembrandt.

122. One Abraham's Sacrifice by Jan Lievens.

123. One *vanitas* retouched by Rembrandt.

124. One landscape in grisaille by Hercules Seghers.

125. One evening scene by Rembrandt.

126. One large mirror.

127. Six chairs with blue seats.

128. One oak table.

129. One embroidered tablecloth

130. One chest of *sackern* [? cedar wood]

131. One ditto *luijerkassie*.

132. One bed and bolster.

133. Two pillows.

134. Two bed covers.

135. One blue bed curtain.

136. One rush-bottom chair.

137. One warming pan.

In the Kunst Caemer [Gallery]

138. Two globes.

139. One box full of minerals.

140. One small column.

141. One small tin pot.

142. One child pissing.

143. Two East Indian cups.

144. One bowl ditto and one Chinese bowl.

145. One statue of an Empress.

120. See no. 27.
121. Probably the small picture in the National Gallery, London, no. 1400.
125. Conceivably the picture in the Dublin Gallery.
131. Hofstede de Groot translates as 'chest for children's clothes'; Charles Blanc as 'a cupboard of marbled wood'.
142. The best known example of this subject in the Netherlands was the statue in Brussels by Jerome Duquesnoy, done in 1619 to replace an earlier fountain of the same subject. Rembrandt could have owned a replica of this, but the motif was not uncommon in the sixteenth century.

146. One East Indian powder-horn.

147. One statue of the Emperor Augustus.

148. One Indian cup.

149. One statue of Tiberius.

150. One East Indian work-box.

151. One head of Caius.

152. One Caligula.

153. Two porcelain *caguwarisen* [?]

154. One Heraclites.

155. Two small figures in porcelain.

156. One Nero.

157. Two iron helmets.

158. One Japanese helmet.

159. One *carbaetse* [? Carpathian] helmet.

160. One Roman Emperor.

161. One head of a Moor cast from life.

162. One Socrates.

163. One Homer.

164. One Aristotle.

165. One antique head.

166. One Faustina.

167. One iron armour and helmet.

168. One Emperor Galba.

169. One ditto Otto.

170. One ditto Vitellius.

171. One ditto Vespasian.

172. One ditto Titus Vespasianus.

173. One ditto Domitian.

174. One ditto Silius Brutus.

175. Forty seven specimens of land and sea creatures, and things of that sort.

176. Twenty three specimens of sea and land animals.

147. For Rembrandt's series of busts of Roman emperors, see p. 77.

153. The word *caguwarisen*, not in any dictionary, is said to mean cassowaries.

159. *Carbaetse* has defeated all translators.

161. Life casts were much used for teaching students up to the end of the nineteenth century, cf. also nos. 178, 316, 317.

200

177. One *hammach*[? hammock] with two *kalbassen*[? metal attachments in the shape of a gourd], one of copper
178. Eight large pieces of plaster work, cast from life.

On the Shelf at the back

179. A great quantity of shells, marine specimens, plasters, plaster casts from life and many other varieties.
180. One figure representing an antique cupid.
181. One hand gun and one pistol.
182. One iron shield decorated with figures by Quintin the Smith, a rare piece.
183. One old fashioned powder horn.
184. One Turkish powder horn.
185. One cabinet of medals.
186. One engraved shield.
187. Two completely naked figures.
188. One cast of the head of Prince Maurice done after his death.
189. One lion and a bull modelled from life.
190. Several walking sticks.
191. One arbalest.

A Set of Art Books

192. One book containing sketches by Rembrandt.
193. One book with woodcuts by Lucas van Leyden.
194. One ditto woodcuts by Was.... [last letters illegible]
195. One ditto with copper-plate engravings by Vanni as well as Baroccio.
196. One ditto with copper-plate engravings by[after] Raphael of Urbino.

177. If *hammach* really means hammock, *kalbassen* [gourds] is hard to explain.
185. Rembrandt's interest in medals is proved by his use of Pisanello's Gian Francesco Gonzaga in the later states of his etching of the Three Crosses [Munz 223] & a drawing of a medal [Benesch, 1186].
195. Francesco Vanni, 1563–1610, and Federigo Baroccio, 1526–1612, were two of the 'proto-baroque' painters who undoubtedly influenced Rembrandt, e.g. the etching of the Virgin Seated in the Clouds [Munz 212] seems to be influenced by Baroccio's etching of the same subject, B. 2.
196. The first of the great collection of engravings after Raphael which influenced Rembrandt so profoundly, see also 205, 206, 214.

197. One small gilt *ledekantie* modelled by Verhulst.
198. One ditto containing copper-plate engravings by Lucas van Leyden double and single impressions.
199. One ditto with drawings by the leading masters of the whole world.
200. The precious book of Andrea Mantegna.
201. One large ditto containing drawings and prints by many masters.
202. Yet another of the same even larger.
203. One ditto containing curious drawings in miniature together with wood and copper prints of all kinds.
204. One ditto containing prints of Breughel the elder.
205. One ditto with prints after Raphael of Urbino.
206. One ditto with prints after the same, very valuable.
207. One ditto containing prints by Antonio Tempesta.
208. One ditto containing prints by Lucas Cranach, both woodcuts and copper plates.
209. One ditto of Annibale, Agostino and Ludovico Carracci, Guido Reni, and Spagnaletto.
210. One ditto with engraved and etched figures by Antonio Tempesta.
211. One ditto with a large book of the same.
212. One ditto book as above.
213. One ditto with engraved copper-plate prints of portraits by Goltzius and Muller.
214. One ditto after Raphael of Urbino, very fine impressions.
215. One ditto with drawings by Adrian Brouwer.
216. One ditto, very large with almost all the work of Titian.
217. Severl rare cups in Venetian glass.

197. Probably Rombaut Verhulst, 1624–1698, a Hague craftsman-carver. The usual translation is 'a small gilded bedstead' but this could not have been included in the set of art books. Probably it was a carved binding, as Verhulst also did ivory carving.
200. See page 147.
204. The only example I have found of Rembrandt making direct use of Breughel's prints is the figure of Christ writing on the ground in the drawing of Christ and the Adulteress in Stockholm, see p. 180.
207. Antonio Tempesta, 1555–1630, a prolific painter and engraver in the late Roman mannerist style.
213. Hendrick Goltzius, 1558–1617, painter and engraver a leading figure in the Haarlem school of mannerists. His engraved portraits are chiefly early works.

218. One antique book with a collection of sketches by Rembrandt.

219. One antique book.

220. One large book containing sketches by Rembrandt.

221. Yet another antique book empty.

222. One small tric-trac board.

223. One very old chair.

224. One Chinese bowl containing minerals.

225. One large lump of white coral.

226. One book of statues engraved on copper.

227. One ditto of engravings by Heemskerk, containing all his works.

228. One book full of portraits, as of Van Dyck, Rubens and various other old masters.

229. One ditto full of landscapes by various masters.

230. One ditto full of the work of Michelangelo Buonarotti.

231. Two small woven baskets.

232. One book with erotica by Raphael, Rosso, Anibale Carracci and Giulio Bonasone.

233. One ditto containing landscapes by various esteemed masters.

234. One ditto containing Turkish buildings by Melchior Lorch, Hendrick van Aelst and others, illustrating Turkish life.

235. One East Indian *benneken*, [basket, but here probably small box] containing various prints by Rembrandt, Hollar, Cock and others.

236. One book bound in black leather with the best sketches of Rembrand.

237. One *papiere kas* [cardboard box or paper folder] full of prints by Martin Schongauer, Holbein, Hans Brosmar and Israel van Mecken.

238. Yet another book with all the works of Rembrandt.

239. One book containing drawings by Rembrandt representing naked men and women.

227. Marten van Heemskerk, 1498–1574, painter and engraver, founder of the Haarlem school of mannerists.

230. Engravings after Michelangelo presumably included the Antonio da Salamanca print of the Julius Monument; see page 92.

232. The *erotica* 'by Raphael' were probably the well-known engravings by Marcantonio after Giulio Romano, B. 231, for which Aretino wrote his even more indecent sonnets.

234. Melchior Lorch or Lorichs, 1527–1583 [?], German engraver, was in Constantinople in 1559 when he did a number of engravings of architecture.

240. One ditto containing drawings of Roman buildings and views by eminent masters.

241. One East Indian basket full of casts and heads.

242. One empty album.

243. One ditto as above.

244. One ditto containing landscapes drawn from nature by Rembrandt.

245. One ditto with trial proofs [after pictures] by Rubens and Jordaens.

246. One ditto full of portraits by van Mierevelt, Titian and others.

247. One small Chinese basket.

248. One ditto [album] containing prints of architecture.

249. One ditto containing prints by Frans Floris, Buyteweg, Goltzius, and Abraham Bloemaert.

250. One ditto containing drawings by Rembrandt representing animals done from life.

251. One parcel of drawings from the antique by Rembrandt.

252. Five small books in quarto full of drawings by Rembrandt.

253. One ditto full of prints of architecture.

254. Medea, a tragedy by Jan Six.

255. Gant's Jerusalem by Jacques Callot.

256. One book bound in parchment full of landscapes drawn from life.

257. One ditto full of figure sketches by Rembrandt.

257a. One ditto as above.

258. One small book with a wooden binding containing *teljooren* [dishes]

259. One small book containing views drawn by Rembrandt.

260. One ditto containing outstanding examples of calligraphy.

---

240. This with 248 and 253 suggest the source from which Rembrandt derived the elaborate architecture that appears in the background of several of his pictures, e.g., Return of the Prodigal Son in the Hermitage.

246. The portraits of Mierevelt would be in the engravings of W. J. Delf.

249. Three of the most extreme exponents of northern mannerism, whose stylishness might not have seemed to Rembrandt's taste, but whom he presumably valued for their inventiveness.

254. The first edition contained the fourth state of Rembrandt's etching of the Marriage of Jason and Creusa, Munz, 270, although in fact this scene does not occur in Six's drama.

258. *teljooren* means a plate, saucer or dish. The book may have contained designs for ornamental dishes.

261. One book full of drawings of statues by Rembrandt done 'from life'.

262. One ditto as above.

263. One ditto containing sketches drawn with the pen by Pieter Lastman.

264. One ditto by Lastman, but in red chalk.

265. One ditto of sketches drawn by Rembrandt with the pen.

266. One ditto as above.

267. One ditto as before.

268. Yet another ditto of the same.

269. Yet another ditto of the same.

270. One large ditto [album] with drawings of the Tyrol by Roelant Savery drawn from nature.

271. One ditto containing drawings by various famous masters.

272. One ditto *in quarto* containing sketches by Rembrandt.

273. Albrecht Dürer's book on proportion with woodcuts.

274. Yet another scrap-book with prints, including the work of Jan Lievens and Ferdinand Bol.

275. Some parcels of sketches by Rembrandt and others.

276. A quantity of large sheets of paper.

277. One box with prints by Van Vliet after paintings by Rembrandt.

278. One Spanish screen covered with material.

279. One iron gorget.

280. One drawer in which there is a bird of Paradise and six fans.

281. Fifteen books of various sizes.

---

263. A number of Rembrandt's copies of Lastman's drawings in red chalk have survived; cf. Benesch, vol. II, 205, 446, 447, 448, 449.

270. The Blauer Atlas in the Court Library at Vienna contains large views of the Tyrol by Roelant Savery, which have been pasted in, so could be the same as those owned by Rembrandt.

273. The book is entitled *Underweysung der Messung*, Nürnberg, 1525, The woodcut in the fourth book of an artist drawing a portrait influenced Rembrandt.

277. Joris van Vliet, 1610–1635, was a coarse but prolific etcher who joined Rembrandt in about 1630 and is responsible for some of the etchings published from his studio. He probably completed several of Rembrandt's own plates. e.g. The Good Samaritan, and also did a number of large etchings reproducing his work, c.f. Munz Vol II, p. 169.

280. Rembrandt's drawing of the bird-of-paradise is in the Louvre, Collection Bonnat, Benesch no. 456, datable about 1640.

282. One book in high Dutch [i.e. German] with military subjects.
283. One ditto with woodcuts.
284. One Josephus in high Dutch, filled with pictures by Tobias Stimmer.
285. One old Bible.
286. One small marble ink-stand.
287. A plaster cast of Prince Maurice.

The Ante-chamber before the Gallery

288. One Joseph by Aertie van Leyden.
289. Three framed prints.
290. The Annunciation.
291. One small landscape painted from nature by Rembrandt.
292. One small landscape by Hercules Seghers.
293. The Descent from the Cross by Rembrandt.
294. One head, from the life.
295. One death's head, painted over by Rembrandt.
296. One plaster of Diana bathing, by Adam van Vianne.
297. One study of a model from life.
298. Two little dogs done from the life, by Titus van Rhyn.
299. One book of pictures by the same.
300. One head of the Virgin Mary by the same.
301. One small moonlight landscape, over-painted by Rembrandt.
302. One copy after the scourging of Christ, by Rembrandt.
303. One small nude study of a woman, done from a model by Rembrandt.
304. One small unfinished landscape by the same.
305. One horse, from the life, by the same.

284. Tobias Stimmer, 1539–1584, a German illustrator, craftsman and designer active in Strasbourg. His illustrated edition of Josephus with 111 woodcuts was published in Strasbourg in 1574.
287. Either another cast of the death-mask mentioned in 188, or possibly a life-mask.
293. This cannot be the picture in Munich which was in the possession of the House of Orange: the picture in the Hermitage is more probably no. 37 in this inventory.
299. *geschildert boeck* an unusual form, which suggests that this was not a book of drawings, but perhaps of small paintings in gouache or watercolour. No painting of Titus can be identified, but there are several signed drawings, cf. Welcker in *Oud Holland*, vol. LV, 1938, p. 268.

306. One small piece by the young Hals.
307. One small fish from life.
308. One bowl modelled in plaster with naked figure, by Adam van Vian.
309. One old chest.
310. Four chairs with black leather seats.
311. One deal table.

In the Small Painting Room in the First Case

312. Thirty-three pieces of ancient weapons and wind instruments.

In the Second Case

313. Thirty-three pieces of ancient hand weapons, arrows, staffs, assegais and bows.

In the Third Case

314. Thirteen pieces of bamboo wind instruments and fifes.

In the Fourth Case

315. Thirteen pieces of arrows, bows, shields, etcetera.

In the Fifth Case

316. A large collection of hands and heads cast from life., together with a harp and a Turkish bow.

In the Sixth Case

317. Seventeen hands and arms, cast from life.
318. A collection of stags' horns.
319. Four bows and cross-bows.
320. Five old helmets and shields.

306. Either Frans Hals' younger brother, Dirk, or one of his sons.
308. Adam van Vian, an Utrecht goldsmith, c. 1569–1627.

321. Nine gourds and bottles.

322. Two sculptured heads portraying Barthel Beham and his wife.

323. One plaster cast of a Greek antique.

324. One statue of the Emperor Agrippa.

325. Ditto of the Emperor Aurelius.

326. One head of Christ, a study from life.

327. One satyr's head, with horns.

328. One antique Sibyl.

329. One antique Laocoön.

330. One large marine plant.

331. One Vitellius.

332. One Seneca.

333. Three or four antique heads of women.

334. Another four heads.

335. One small metal cannon.

336. A collection of antique stuffs of various colours.

337. Seven stringed instruments.

338. Two little pictures by Rembrandt.

In the Large Painting Room

339. Twenty pieces, including halberds, swords and Indian fans.

340. One [pair of] costumes for an Indian man and woman.

341. One giant's helmet.

342. Five cuirasses.

343. One wooden trumpet.

344. Two Moors, in one picture, by Rembrandt.

345. One little child by Michelangelo.

322. Barthel Beham, the German painter and engraver, 1502–1540, together with his brother Hans Sebald Beham, was one of the minor German engravers whose use of perspective seems to have influenced Rembrandt.

344. This cannot be the well-known picture of the subject in the Mauritshius, which is dated 1661.

345. Either a cast of the famous sleeping cupid in Mantua or of the Child in the Bruges Madonna.

On the Picture Rack

346. The skins of a lion and a lioness, with two coloured coats.
347. One large piece representing Danae.
348. One peacock by Rembrandt, from the life.

In the Small Cupboard

349. Ten pieces of painting, both large and small, by Rembrandt.
350. One bedstead.

In the Small Kitchen

351. One tin waterpot.
352. Several pots and pans.
353. One small table.
354. One food cupboard.
355. Various old chairs.
356. Two chair cushions.

In the Passage

357. Nine white cups.
358. Two earthenware plates.

Linen at the Laundry

359. Three man's shirts.
360. Six handkerchiefs.
361. Twelve knapkins.
362. Three tablecloths.
363. Several collars and cuffs.

done and inventoried on the 25th and 26th July, 1656.

---

347. It is tempting to identify this 'large piece' with the famous picture in The Hermitage. Against this it must be observed 1) that over the word Danae in a different ink is written the correction *Dianae*; 2) that Rembrandt is not named as the painter, as he is in all other items where his work is listed.

A Short List of the Chief Books and Articles Used

Names in capitals are used in references.

BENESCH or BEN	[in references to drawings] Otto Benesch, *The Drawings of Rembrandt*. London. vols. I and II, 1954; vols. III and IV, 1955; vols. V and VI, 1957.
M. D. Henkel	*Catalogus van de Nederlandsche Teekeningen en het Rijksmuseum te Amsterdam. I Teekeningen van Rembrandt en zijn School*. s'Gravenhage 1942.
C. Hofstede de Groot	*Catalogue of Dutch Painters*, vol. VI, *Rembrandt*. London 1916.
LUGT, INVENTAIRE	*Musée du Louvre, Inventaire Général des Écoles du Nord;* École Hollandaise par Frits Lugt, vol. III, *Rembrandt*, Paris 1933.
Frits Lugt	"Italiaansche Kunstwerken in Nederlandsche Verzamlingen" in *Oud Holland*, LIII (1936) pp. 97–135.
MACLAREN	*National Gallery Catalogues, The Dutch School* by Neil Maclaren. London, 1960.
MUNZ	Ludwig Munz, *Rembrandt's Etchings* vols. I and II. London, 1952.
Ludwig Munz	*Rembrandt's Alterstil und die Barockklassik; Rembrandt's Korrekturen an Schülerzeichnungen nach 1650. Jahrbuch der Kunsthistorischen Sammlungen*, Neue Folge 9, Wien [1935], p. 201.
Carl Neumann	*Aus der Werkstatt Rembrandts*. Heidelberg, 1918.
RIJCKVORSEL	Rijckvorsel *Rembrandt en de Traditie*, 1932.
ROSENBERG	Jakob Rosenberg, *Rembrandt*. Cambridge, Mass, 1948.
Jakob Rosenberg	Reviews of *Benesch*. The Art Bulletin, March 1957 and March 1959.
SAXL	Fritz Saxl, *Rembrandt and Classical Antiquity* in *Lectures* vol. I, p. 298. London, 1957.
SLIVE	Seymour Slive, *Rembrandt and his Critics 1630–1730*. The Hague, 1953.
URKUNDEN	C. Hofstede de Groot, *Urkunden über Rembrandt*. s'Gravenhage, 1906.
VALENTINER or VAL	[in references to drawings] W. R. Valentiner, *Die Handzeichnungen Rembrandts*. Stuttgart, vol. I.
W. R. Valentiner	*Rembrandt und seine Umgebung*. Strasbourg, 1905.

210

Notes

Chapter 1 (pages 1 to 40)

1. The original passage, which can hardly be rendered literally, reads 'Rembrantum judico et affectuum vivacitate Livio praestare, hunc alteri inventionis et quadam audacium argumentorum formarumque superbia.' cf. J. A. Worp, *Bijdragen en Mededeelingen van het Historisch Genootschap*, XVIII, 1897, p. 77.

2. E.g. an etching by Van Vliet, dated 1634, and another by Hollar purporting to depict Heraclitus and Democritus; cf. Seymour Slive, *Rembrandt and his Critics*, 1953, pls. 13, 14, 15.

3. The only drawings of the seventeenth century which seem to anticipate Rembrandt's violently expressive style are those of Elsheimer. His sketch-book in Frankfurt, which was probably executed before Rembrandt was born, contains drawings so close in style to Rembrandt that it is hard to believe they were not known to him. He was also much influenced by the bold and lively style of Callot.

4. They are those of Joachim von Sandrart, 1675, cf. p. 30; Filippo Baldinucci, 1686; and Arnold Houbraken, 1718. They are accessible to the general reader in *Rembrandt*, (Phaidon Press editions).

5. Cf. Fritz Saxl, *Lectures*, 1957, Vol. I, p. 299.

6. The sketch in oils is in the Petit Palais, Paris.

7. Cf. Saxl, op. cit., p. 303.

8. However, he owned two books of engravings by Goltzius and one of Bloemaert, Floris, and Buyteweg, listed in the inventory, nos. 213 and 249.

8ª. It is just possible that he had seen a picture of the subject, of which at least two replicas are in existence, one in Hampton Court, no. 297, the other in the Kunsthistorisches Museum, Vienna, no. 95, engraved in Tenier's *Theatrum Pictoricum*, that belonged to Archduke Leopold Wilhelm, Governor of the Spanish Netherlands.

9. A copy of finer quality in Windsor, cat. no. 457, which long passed as the original, shows only the upper half, with the figure of Ganymede; on the other hand, the coloured drawing in a style reminiscent of Giulio Clovio in the Casa Buonarotti shows the landscape and one dog.

10. As an example of the curious ambivalence with which Michelangelo and his circle regarded antique myths, cf. a letter of Sebastiano del Piombo, Milanesi, *Corr.*, p. 104, quoted in de Tolnay, *The Medici Chapel* (Princeton, 1948, p. 50) in which he suggests that Michelangelo should turn his Ganymede into a St. John the Evangelist being taken to heaven by his symbolic eagle, and use it in the cupola of the sacristy of San Lorenzo.

11. No. 32, now ascribed to Damiano Mazza. It seems to have been in the Palazzo Colonna, Rome (as a Titian) till bought by Angerstein in 1801. It is so superior to the only known work of Mazza that I incline to think it reproduces a design by Titian, which Rembrandt may have known.

12. His attitude seems to have been derived from a figure in Pietro Testa's etching of a boar-hunt, cf. Rijckvorsel, *Rembrandt en de Traditie*, 1932, p. 129.

13. In fact, he does seem to be wearing a kilt and plaid, no doubt derived from a classical representation of a barbarian.

14. Shortly before, he had painted a grisaille of the same subject, now in the Rijksmuseum, which is a redolently local performance. Rembrandt's understanding of Baroque may be said to date from between these two pictures.

15. The device of people sitting like an audience in the box of a theatre is common in Rembrandt's work, and probably reflects his known enthusiasm for the stage. Examples are the etchings of the Triumph of Mordecai, Christ Among the Doctors (of 1654), and the Execution of St. John the Baptist.

16. For the high renaissance origins of the design, cf. p. 90 below.

17. The one drawing in which Rembrandt, following renaissance tradition, relates human proportion to a square, shows the figure fully dressed in Turkish costume. It is in the Louvre, and doubted by Lugt, Inv. 1301, but I am inclined to accept it.

18. A famous figure of a damned soul in Michelangelo's Last Judgement, with one eye covered and the other staring into space, makes a similar effect of half-crazy despair, and may have been the source of Rembrandt's idea.

19. Usually said to have been influenced by the figures of Adam and Eve in Dürer's engraving of the Harrowing of Hell, B. 41, but the likeness is not close enough to be convincing.

20. An engraving of the Leyden Anatomical Theatre is published by Julius Held in his admirable article on the Polish Rider in *The Art Bulletin*, Vol. XVI, 1944, pp. 246–265.

21. Benesch 728, maintains that on stylistic grounds the drawing cannot be dated later than 1649. Even if this were true (and it is impossible to be so dogmatic) Rembrandt might well have used it for the Polish Rider. Benesch's contention that the drawing is connected with the Quintus Fabius Maximus in Bucharest and the equestrian portrait in London is obviously incorrect. Scholars are unanimous in dating the Polish Rider about 1655.

22. A skeleton horseman in the anatomical theatre in Delft was dressed in Indian costume and trappings; cf. Held, *loc. cit.*, p. 261.

23. I incline to think that Rembrandt has used the same model who posed for Potiphar's Wife in two pictures of 1656 (Berlin and Washington) and in two drawings, in the British Museum and Dresden, Ben. 1174 and 1185.

Chapter 2 (pages 41 to 84)

1. From 1632 to 1633 van Uylenburgh, as well as being a dealer, conducted a sort of art school in which young artists copied the pictures in his possession.

2. cf. Appendix I.

3. Although it is the aim of this book to show Rembrandt's debt to the Italian Renaissance, I must not give the impression that he was uninfluenced by the Bolognese and earlier mannerists, in particular by illustrators like Stradanus, Vaenius, Marten van Heemskerk, Marten de Vos, Buyteweg and Bloemaert. But, like Lucas van Leyden, they were chiefly a source of iconographical motives, and did not influence his style.

4. Perhaps there was a special reason why Rembrandt valued this print so highly, since it shows how Raphael dealt with the problem of artificial light.

5. In a masterly review in *The Art Bulletin*, vol. XLI, 1959, p. 108.

6. All his life Rembrandt tended to grow impatient with foreshortened arms, and often gives them a curious relationship to the body. Cf. the drawing of a woman in the British Museum (Ben. 1174) datable about 1656.

7. Benesch, no. 475, believes that although the drawing is by Bol, the square lines round the head of Pharoah's daughter were added by Rembrandt, but they seem to be in the same ink as the other heavy lines in the drawing. This is the kind of trick that a pupil could easily imitate.

8. Large copies of the Last Supper were not unknown in northern Europe, and early drawings of the composition are very common (four in the Louvre alone). Rembrandt may also have seen copies of individual groups or figures, such as the series of drawings at Weimar or the watercolours in Strasbourg.

9. This group was so popular that it was printed as a separate etching. Another group of Pharisees derived from the Last Supper is in the etching of Christ Among the Doctors (Munz, 222).

10. The two paintings of the Supper at Emmaus by Titian, which also go back to Leonardo, do not seem to have been known to Rembrandt at this date, although one of them was later to influence his etching of 1656.

11. *Trattato della Pittura*, ed. A. Borzelli, 1924, § 90.

12. *Trattato* § 143.

13. A number of manuscripts of the *Trattato* were made under Poussin's supervision, and illustrated by copies of his own drawings and diagrams. The master copy seems to be the one in the Hermitage. The Sandrart copy is lost. The printed edition contained engravings based on the Poussin illustrations, but with additions and embellishments which drove him to fury. See Kate Trauman Steinitz *Leonardo da Vinci's Trattato della Pittura*, 1958, pp. 70–94 and 145–150. Some of Poussin's works were evidently known in Rembrandt's studio. Two drawings of the Death of Abel (Valentiner 5 and 6) suggest a Poussin design. The former is a pupil's work, but the latter is authentic. A coarse pupil's drawing in the Louvre (Valentiner 441) representing the Last Supper with the apostles reclining *all'antica* is clearly derived from Poussin's Eucharist in the Ellesmere Sacraments. But it appears to be a Hoogstraten, and if so would have been done after he left Rembrandt.

14. Doubted by Benesch, Cat. no. A 18; accepted by Valentiner, no. 763. Of a type much imitated, but on balance I believe it to be genuine.

15. There is an obviously Leonardesque head in the drawing of Christ preaching in the Louvre (Lugt *Inventaire* 1132), but the authenticity of this drawing is questionable.

16. In the Fogg Catalogue (no. 193) as Perino del Vaga. But the original must certainly have been a Polidoro. Cf. Popham in *Burlington Magazine*, XC, 1948, p. 179.

17. It is accepted by both Valentiner (504) and Benesch (1209). This is a good example of how authenticity should be, and can be, determined by ordinary tests of quality.

18. Jan van Gelder, in *Studies in Western Art: Acts of the Twentieth International Congress of the History of Art*, Princeton, 1962, p. 51.

19. See Van Gelder, *ibid*.

20. Notably Watteau, in his garden statues. On a lower level, Rowlandson enjoyed bringing his statues to life under the noses of his connoisseurs.

21. For example, he bought only a small proportion of the le Blon consignment. The whole was valued at 6,400 florins, Rembrandt's purchases from it cost him 186 florins.

22. An earlier collection by Perrier, with the same title, published in 1638, contains nothing but statues in the round, and does not seem to have influenced Rembrandt. The influence of Perrier's engravings was first pointed out by Hendrick Bramsen, *Burlington Magazine*, XCII, 1950, pp. 128–31.

23. The intention of this relief is mysterious. It is not a sarcophagus motive, and is rather too spread-out in design to be a Greek grave relief. I can find no parallel in antique art yet it does not look like a Renaissance imitation.

Chapter 3 (pages 85 to 100)

1. It was cut down when the picture was transferred to the Town Hall of Amsterdam in 1715, in order that it might fit between two windows.

2. No. 289, usually attributed to Gerritt Lundens. The complex problems of its date and authorship are discussed by Neil Maclaren in the *National Gallery Catalogues*, *The Dutch School* (1960). There is no doubt that it is an accurate copy of the Night Watch before it was cut down.

3. Inv. no. 13733. It was attributed to Rembrandt by Oskar Fischel, and published as such by A. P. Oppé in *Old Master Drawings*, 1939–40, p. 59, pl. 52. At first sight the touch looks too vague and diffuse for Rembrandt himself, but we know how uncertain he could be when making a copy, and his authorship is not entirely excluded.

4. It is fair to say that Prince Frederick Henry continued to employ Rembrandt after Huygens had lost interest in him. But he died in 1647.

5. This print also influenced an engraving by Nicholas de Bruyn dated 1618 and an etching by Callot (Lieure 285) both of which may have been known to Rembrandt. He owned a large collection of Lucas van Leyden's engravings—Inv. nos. 193 (woodcuts) and 198 (copper) and frequently referred to them

6. Most scholars regard this as a preliminary sketch. I believe it to be a note of how the picture should be framed, with alternative mouldings on either side. If so, it would have been done at a time when the picture was nearing completion, and so must be considered as evidence, however slight, of the final appearance of the composition. Rembrandt took trouble about the framing of his pictures, and a drawing in the Louvre (Lugt Inv. 1131) shows the frame for the Preaching of John the Baptist. In this the treatment of the figures is more schematic, partly because the picture had been painted long before, and partly because the whole drawing is more circumstantial and precise. Further evidence of how he wished his pictures framed is provided by the Holy Family at Cassel (fig. 62). As is usual in the matter of frames, posterity has ignored his wishes, and put his pictures into whatever frames were suggestive of wealth and fashion.

7. There is another version which Hans Tietze, *Art in America*, XXIX, 1941, pp. 51–56, published as the original *modello;* and other replicas exist.

8. cf. William S. Heckscher, *Rembrandt's Anatomy of Dr. Nicolaas Tulp*, New York, 1958. The Amsterdam anatomy school was on the upper floor of St. Margaret's Church.

9. Like much else in Jakob Rosenberg, *Rembrandt*, 1948, p. 81, this example cannot be bettered.

214

10. At the official dedication the poet Joost van Vondel composed a rhymed description of the entire building, including the decorative paintings. In fact the structure had only risen to the second storey.

11. Or almost. A book entitled *Batavorum cum Romanis bellum*, published in 1612 with illustrations by Otto Vaenius, engraved by Antonio Tempesta, was evidently known to Rembrandt, since he adapted one of the compositions for his Samson's Wedding Feast in Dresden; cf. H. van de Waal, "The iconological background of Rembrandt's Civilis," in *Konsthistorisk Tidskrift*, XXV, 1956, pp. 12 to 16.

12. It should, however, be noted that Rembrandt seems to have made the figures more grotesque when he re-worked the surviving fragment at the end of his life; cf. the X-rays published by Carl Nordenfalk in *Konsthistorisk Tidskrift*, XXV, 1956, pp. 30 *et seq*.

13. Cf. the excellent study of Seymour Slive, *Rembrandt and his Critics*, The Hague, 1953. For the arguments about the return of the Claudius Civilis, see Wolfgang Stechow, *Art Bulletin* XXXIII, 1941, pp. 227–228.

Chapter 4 (pages 101 to 145)

1. One example usually quoted is the etching of the Supper at Emmaus (1654) where the noble and fatherly figure of Christ, in contrast to the sacrificial figure in the picture of 1648, is clearly inspired by Titian's painting of the subject now in the Louvre, which is known to have been in Amsterdam at the time.
Another is the etching of the Virgin with the Instruments of the Passion (fig. 100), which is similar to several surviving Titians of a Mater Dolorosa. This is perhaps the closest Rembrandt ever came to an actual imitation of an Italian painting, although the addition of the Instruments of the Passion is unusual in Venetian art and Rembrandt may have had in mind a Spanish picture inspired by Titian.

2. Now in the British Museum. Published by Tancred Borenius, *The Picture Gallery of Andrea Vendramin*, London, 1923.

3. *216 Een dito (boeck) seer groot, met meest alle wercken van Titiaen.*

4. Published by Vitale Block in *Apollo*, October 1964, p. 294.

5. *The National Gallery Catalogues, Italian Sixteenth Century, Venetian School*, lists four versions. Another is in the Prado. If Rembrandt saw an original it could have been that in the Arundel Collection, listed in the inventory of 1651 (cf. Mary F.S. Harvey, *Thomas Howard, Earl of Arundel*, 1921, p. 475). But more probably he knew an engraving.

6. Even in this unclassical scene one figure, the running shepherd in the foreground, has a Hellenistic movement, and may be a memory of the angel in Raphael's Heliodorus.

7. It is often assumed that no. 347 of the inventory, *Een groot Stuck Danae*, refers to the Hermitage picture. But as the entry is corrected in ink to *Dianae* and since Rembrandt's name is not mentioned, the identification is by no means certain. A large picture described as *Dane* was in the collection of the widow of Edouart van Domselaer in Amsterdam.

8. The only exception is that curious exercise in the genre of Ostade, the Holy Family of 1640 in the Louvre.

9. Published by Benesch (no. 1369), who says it was recognised by Edith Hoffmann. I have not seen the original, but in reproduction the hypothesis is convincing.

215

10. Almost the only exception is a drawing of the Rest in the Flight belonging to the Norton Simon Foundation (Ben. 965) (fig. 102).

11. This is no place to discuss the influence of the youthful Giorgione on the aged Bellini, but it should be noted that there are instances of the pathetic fallacy in Giovanni Bellini's work dating from before Giorgione's childhood.

12. This was first proposed by Adolfo Venturi, *Storia dell'arte italiana*, Vol IX, 3, p. 494, and has no documentary confirmation. The landscape in the print was probably added by Campagnola.

13. This seems to be the first recorded Venetian night piece, and the forerunner of Savoldo. How far Rembrandt's night pieces such as the beautiful Rest in the Flight in Dublin owed anything to the Venetians it is hard to say. Probably he absorbed their lessons indirectly through Elsheimer.

14. Neither of these could have been known to Rembrandt in the original, but copies of both exist, e.g. a picture reproduced in Richter's *Giorgione*, Chicago, 1937, pl. 74.

15. The colour and tonality of the Castiglione is almost the same as Giorgione's picture of an old woman inscribed *Col Tempo*, now in the Venice Academy.

16. Cecil Gould in *National Gallery Catalogues, The Sixteenth Century, Venetian School, 1959*.

17. One, with a landscape, in Berlin (Cat. no. 197a); another, in which the lady is playing a lute, is at Alnwick, Northumberland. Both are currently ascribed to Palma.

18. A very similar pair of embracing lovers appears in a Venetian picture in the National Gallery, London (no. 1123) traditionally ascribed to Giorgione. It could be the echo of a lost Giorgione design, but more probably it also derives from the Raphael-Giulio Romano group in the Loggia.

19. The likeness between the Jewish Bride and the porphyry Tetrarchs of St. Mark's can only be coincidental. Nevertheless it is worth noting that Rembrandt knew one of these figures, from a woodcut in a book which was certainly in his possession, the *Habiti Antichi e Moderni* of Cesare Vecellio, Venice, 1598.

20. Giorgione's Lovers still existed in the Borghese Collection in 1773 when it was engraved by Domenico Cunego, cf. Bernard Berenson, *Venetian Painters*, illustrated edition, 1957, vol. II, pl. 681.

21. No. 221, with tentative attribution to Callisto da Lodi or Romanino. Berenson lists it as Domenico Mancini but Mancini's signed altar-piece in Lendinara is dated 1511, which would seem to me at least ten years too early for the Dresden Lovers.

22. For de Piles' comparison of Rembrandt and Titian, cf. Seymour Slive, *op. cit.*, pp. 131–2.

Chapter 5 *(pages 146 to 190)*

1. Accepted by Hind and Rosenberg; Benesch (A. 105a) expresses some doubt on the grounds that the preparatory outlines are in red chalk. But Rembrandt's copy of the Last Supper in the Lehman Collection is also redrawn over a rather timid under-drawing in red chalk.

2. Rejected by Benesch (A. 93), accepted by Rosenberg. Obviously related to a drawing of Susanna Brought to Judgement in the Ashmolean Museum, Oxford (same size and date), and so perhaps preparatory to a series of decorative paintings of biblical heroines

3. The nearest design is a painting ascribed to Mantegna in the Goodbody Collection, Invergarry, Scotland. Rembrandt also owned a medal of Andrea Doria, of which the, original cannot be traced. He copied it in a drawing in Berlin, Ben. 1186

4. In Berlin and the Louvre, Ben. 180, 179.

5. The large decorative paintings in the new Town Hall of Amsterdam (see p. 97) were in this form.

6. For example by Benesch (543) and Lugt (*Inventaire, 1132*). It was doubted by Demonts, *Les accroissements du Louvre en 1920*, pl. 23, and, although not entirely convinced, I can see the force of his opinion. If it is not authentic it must be a *pasticcio* done in Rembrandt's studio, and contains motives which were current there; for example the man in profile above the kneeling woman, who is derived from a Leonardo (see above, fig. 70) and the man kneeling to the right, who appears to be taken from Annibale Carracci.

7. In the Morgan Library. Accepted by Valentiner, 622B. It could be by the same hand as a drawing in Stockholm of Christ Before Pilate, Val. 469.

8. It was attributed to Latanzio da Rimini by von Hadeln, *Venezianische Zeichnungen des Quattrocento*, Berlin, 1925, plate 83.

9. This was a drawing for a decoration, destroyed by fire in 1483, in the Sala del Maggior Consiglio in the Doge's Palace. The Italian copy is in the British Museum, cf. A. E. Popham and Philip Pouncey *Italian Drawings in the Department of Prints and Drawings of the British Museum. The Fourteenth and Fifteenth Centuries*, London 1950. no. 9. on p. 6; plate VIII; the Rembrandtesque copy is in the Albertina, inv. no. 8810.

10. Seven of them are now lost, but are known to have been in the collection of Richardson. A majority of the others are in the British Museum; cf. note to Ben. 1187, F. Sarre in *Jahrbuch d. Kgl. Preuss. Kunstslgn.* XXV, 1904, pp. 143–158, and R. Ettinghausen in *De artibus opuscula XL; Essays in Honor of Erwin Panofsky*, New York, 1960.

11. By the Master B with the Dice, dated 1532.

12. It will be observed that Claudius Civilis is wearing a hat of a similar kind.

13. The etching of a landscape with a sportsman and dogs (Hind 265), datable soon after 1650, recalls a Poussin composition by its road receding with a double diagonal, its church tower providing a vertical accent and its strongly modelled hills closing the space.

14. E.g. the Presentation in the Temple in the Louvre (Rothschild Bequest), Ben. 589, which could be 1646/7. The Esau Selling his Birthright, in Amsterdam (Ben. 607), would be an extreme example if Benesch's date, 1647/8, were correct. But it is obviously a drawing of the mid-1650's, and, if ever by Rembrandt, has been entirely made over.

15. The unconvincing perspective of the step in the foreground, which seems to be jutting out into space, is a misunderstanding of a device frequently employed by Dürer, e.g. in his woodcut of the Virgin in the Temple, B. 81.

16. It has been claimed that this etching represents Judas returning (or about to return) the pieces of silver. Judas would be the pensive figure seated in the centre. If true, this would make an interesting contrast to Rembrandt's early picture (fig. 1) but I fear the suggestion is only an instance of iconomania.

17. Nicholas Maes was born in 1634, and by 1652 he was painting the type of interior which was to be perfected in 1656 by de Hooch and Vermeer; and it was probably through him that Rembrandt's ideas of composition spread to the painters of Dordrecht and Delft.

18. The incident is described only in John, VIII, 3–8. It is represented in a grisaille by Breughel in the collection of Count Seilern, which was engraved (Bastelaer, no. III). Rembrandt owned a book of Breughel's engravings (inv. no. 204) and it has hitherto been assumed that this print was the source of Rembrandt's design.

19. The Christ Preaching is undated, but is probably later than Christ Presented to the People of 1655, and is another example of how, after dogmatic work, Rembrandt returned to a more human treatment, where art is more carefully concealed.

20. This figure, who is followed fairly closely in Rembrandt's etching, is entirely different in Marcantonio's engraving of St. Paul Preaching, which proves that in this instance Rembrandt's knowledge of the cartoons came from some other source. The figure on the right of the podium in Christ Presented to the People (fig. 82) is also far closer to the cartoon than to the Marcantonio.

21. c.f. John Pope-Hennessy, *Donatello's Relief of the Ascension with Christ giving the Keys to St. Peter*, London, 1949.

Index

221